Decorations of the
National Society of the Daughters of the American Revolution

President-General

State-Regent
Ex-State-Regent
Honorary State-Regent

Membership Insignia
Pendent

Vice-President General
Ex-Vice-President-
General
Honorary
Vice-President General

Membership Insignia
Pendent

National Officers

Charter-Members

PLATE I

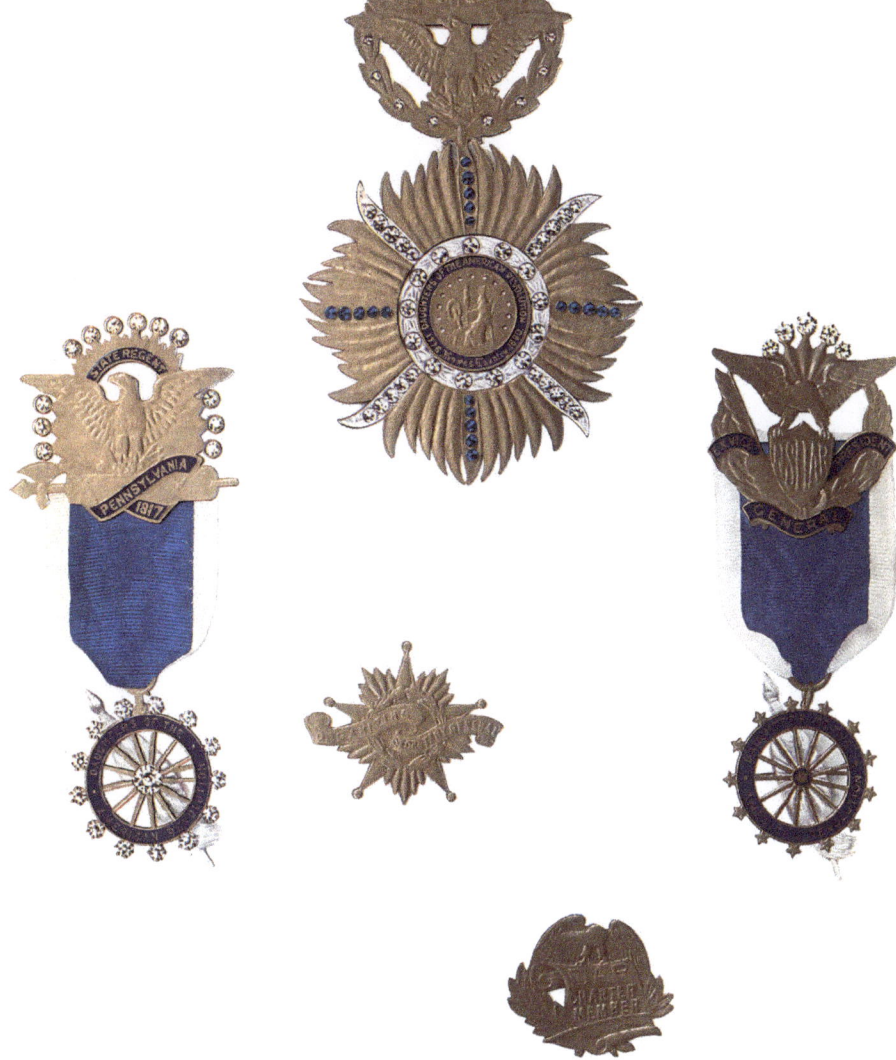

AMERICAN ORDERS & SOCIETIES
AND THEIR DECORATIONS

The Objects of the Military and
Naval Orders, Commemorative
and Patriotic Societies of the
United States and the Requirements for Membership therein

WITH ILLUSTRATIONS IN COLORED RELIEF

Compiled by
JENNINGS HOOD, Manager, Department of Insignia
CHARLES J. YOUNG, Manager, Department of Heraldry

The Naval & Military Press Ltd

Published by

The Naval & Military Press Ltd
Unit 5 Riverside, Brambleside
Bellbrook Industrial Estate
Uckfield, East Sussex
TN22 1QQ England

Tel: +44 (0)1825 749494

www.naval-military-press.com
www.nmarchive.com

THE ORIGIN AND PROPER OCCASIONS FOR WEARING INSIGNIA OF THE VARIOUS MILITARY AND NAVAL ORDERS, ALSO PATRIOTIC AND HISTORIC-COMMEMORATIVE SOCIETIES

The wearing of the insignia on the left breast only, probably evolved from the fact that it was the shield side of the Crusaders, and furthermore, because it was near the loyal heart that the knight placed his badge of honor and fealty to his king.

Where membership is held in more than one order or society, the member should choose the insignia appropriate to the occasion, and if an officer wear around his neck only the emblem of that society which he especially wishes to represent, provided such method of wearing the insignia is sanctioned by the regulations of that society. It is the better custom not to wear at the same time all the insignia a member may possess, but rather to wear those which relate to the occasion. A Colonial Society insignia might be worn at a banquet of the Society of the Revolution to show that one's ancestor had been in the earlier struggle that led to the development of the Colonies, or vice versa. A companion might wear the Naval Order beside the Loyal Legion insignia to emphasize the fact that it was on the sea the service was rendered to his country.

At semi-full-dress affairs or military and naval receptions, the miniature insignia (only issued to those having the larger or official ones) may be worn effectively. They may be pendant from a bar pin, or, when ribbons are removed, may be attached to a gold chain, etc.; one end secured in the buttonhole of lapel and the other end by a stick-pin. Miniature decorations, under no circumstances, should be worn in daily costume, except, perhaps, at a military reception.

Rosettes worn in lieu of decorations are only worn in the left lapel of the coat, one at a time, and never in an overcoat. Insignia are issued to members only, upon authorization sent to the makers, when signed by the chancellor or secretary of the particular organization, and must be numbered, the secretary keeping record of the same. If a member is expelled or resigns,

3

his insignia is expected to be returned; otherwise, it remains an heirloom in his family. Each insignia has its historic and heraldic significance, and in design symbolizes the historic-commemorative or war period it seeks to perpetuate. The ribbons of these orders and societies, by their combination of color, are also emblematic.

Regulations as to the wearing of insignia of the various military and naval orders are prescribed in the constitutions and by-laws. These differ in a few details; the following cover the regulations in all important points:

The insignia should always be worn at the regular meetings of the organization and on any detached or representative duty.

It should never be worn at other times except on "occasions of ceremony," including special commemorations of a national character.

Such occasions of ceremony should be determined by the custom of the Military or Naval Services of the United States, respectively, or, when no such custom exists, by Continental usage.

General Orders No. 48.   War Department,

War Department,
Washington, July 22, 1913.

I.   General Orders, No. 97, War Department, May 12, 1909, as amended by Paragraph II, General Orders, No. 220, War Department, November 1, 1909, and by Paragraph II, General Orders, No. 39, War Department, May 27, 1913, is rescinded and the following substituted therefor:

The following instructions are published relative to the wearing of medals and badges by officers and enlisted men of the Army to whom such medals or badges have been awarded:

1.   The Medal of Honor will be worn on occasions of ceremony whenever the full-dress uniform, the special evening dress, or the mess jacket is worn.   With the full-dress uniform the medal will be worn pendent from the neck, the ribbon passing between the upper and lower hooks of the coat collar, so that the medal proper shall hang about one inch below the opening of the collar.   With the special evening dress or mess jacket the medal will be worn pendent from the neck, the ribbon passing around the neck under the collar, so that the medal proper shall hang about one inch below the tie.

2.   Other medals and badges awarded by the Government will be worn on the left breast of the coat in the following order of precedence, beginning at the right:

a.   Certificate of Merit Badge (issued by the War Department).

b.   Medal commemorating the Battle of Manila Bay (issued by the Navy Department).

c.   Medal commemorating the naval engagements in the West Indies (issued by the Navy Department).

d.   Special meritorious medal for service during the War with Spain, other than in battle (issued by the Navy Department).

e. Philippines Congressional medal (issued by the War Department).

f. Campaign badges, in the order of the dates of the campaigns (issued by War and Navy Departments).

g. Gold life-saving medal (issued by the Treasury Department).

h. Silver life-saving medal (issued by the Treasury Department).

i. Army of Cuban Pacification badge (issued by War and Navy Departments).

j. Good conduct medal (issued by the Navy Department).

k. Aviator's badge (issued by the War Department).

l. Various distinctive marks awarded for excellence in small-arms practice (issued by War and Navy Departments).

m. Medals or badges awarded for service performed while in the Army, Navy or Marine Corps, or other branch of the Government, if not included among those specified above.

3. Officers and enlisted men of the Army are authorized to wear with the uniform any medals or badges awarded to them by the Government during previous service in any other branch of the Government.

4. On all occasions of ceremony where full-dress uniform is prescribed, the medals and badges named in paragraph 1 and in sections a, b, c, d, e, f, g, h, i and j of paragraph 2 of this order will be worn, except as provided in paragraph 6. Officers, including majors, and enlisted men of the Philippine Scouts, will wear the medals and badges specified in this paragraph with the olive drab cotton service uniform on occasions of ceremony.

5. Aviators' badges, the various distinctive marks awarded for excellence in small-arms practice, and the medals and badges referred to in section n, paragraph 2, and in paragraph 3 of this order, may be worn on all occasions, except on active duty in the field in time of war, or during maneuvers.

6

6.   Badges of military societies may be worn on all occasions of ceremony in the following order from right to left, but officers and enlisted men on the active list of the Army will not wear these badges with the badges and medals named in paragraphs 1 and 2:

a.   Badges of military societies commemorative of the wars of the United States, including the Philippine Insurrection and the China Relief Expedition, in the order of the dates of such wars.

b.   Badges of the Regular Army and Navy Union of the United States and of the Army and Navy Union of the United States.

c.   Corps and division badges of the Civil War and the War with Spain.

d.   Badge of the Enlisted Men's Abstinence League.

II.   A rosette will be issued by the Chief of the Quartermaster Corps to each person to whom a Philippines Congressional medal, certificate of merit badge, campaign badge, or Army of Cuban Pacification badge has been or may be awarded, the rosette to be for optional wear with civilian clothing, in lieu of the medal or badge to which it pertains, and to be made of ribbons of the same colors as those that pertain to such medal or badge.

ANCIENT HERALDIC AND CHIVALRIC ORDER OF ALBION

Instituted 1643.   Reorganized 1883

History and Traditions of the Knights of Albion

This Order was instituted originally in 1643 in America, by Sir Edmund Plowden, an English Nobleman of distinguished ancestry, for the conversion of the 23 Indian tribes comprised within the grant of New Albion. Sir Edmund Plowden was by grant of Charles I, created "Lord Earl Palatine of New Albion," which comprised portions of what are now New Jersey, Pennsylvania, Delaware and Virginia. Much of the history of the Order and its members, together with a design representing its seal, insignia and ribbon, is to be found among the historical MSS. of the State of Delaware. After the settlement of the Swedes and Dutch and formation of the Colonies and consequent change of government, the Order became officially inactive. Tradition, however, states that the descendants of the original members kept up the organization of the Order as a private secret society of gentlemen long after the Revolution. Members were admitted to the Society from time to time who were not descendants of original members. After the great conflict the members who remained in the Society formed part of that brilliant entourage of Hamilton and with the other conservative elements, such as the Cincinnati, contributed somewhat to the stability of the government.

It lingered for many years in a more or less moribund condition until 1883, when it was merged as a high degree of Knighthood into what was known as the Patriotic Order of the Fathers and Founders of the Republic, composed of certain gentlemen of distinguished ancestry in Pennsylvania and New York. After lingering for a number of years as the highest circle of this most exclusive Society, the latter was reorganized into the present form of the Order.

Unfortunately because of the former secrecy observed by all members of the Order, it is most difficult to obtain data about the Society after the Revolution. The custom also of signing by letters or by emblems makes it impossible to verify many things in this venerable Order.

Tradition also states that among the Captains (Captains-General) were Alexander Hamilton, John Ross and Major Popham. How these could have been Presidents of the Society at a time when the members most probably did not meet, history does not state. As reorganized, while no changes whatever have been made in the insignia, seal and certain historical features, its membership regulations have been so amended as to bring it within the scope of modern institutions and the requirements of a Republican and patriotic government, while adhering to that original plan adopted by the founders of the first Ancestral and Hereditary Order instituted in America.

Objects

I. To bring together lineal descendants of the original members of the Order and Signers of the Declaration of Independence and for the purpose of teaching reverent regard for their names and history, character and perseverance, deeds and heroism, and that of their descendants.

II. To discover, collect and preserve, records, documents, manuscripts, monuments and history relating to the original Albion Knights and the Signers of the Declaration of Independence, their ancestors and descendants, and to encourage and improve the study of Heraldry in America and knowledge of the history of the Indians.

III. To commemorate and celebrate events connected with the early history of the Order and the Document of American Freedom.

Membership

Membership in the Order is derived upon invitation only, extended by unanimous vote of the Grand Council to lineal descendants (of the male sex above the age of 21) of

I. Sir Edmund Plowden or an original member of the Order.

II. Signers of the Declaration of Independence.

Honorary Membership

Such membership may be conferred by unanimous vote of the Grand Council upon persons who have rendered unusual services to the cause of science, literature, history or art, in public or official life, or in recognition of special services rendered to Country, or upon the male descendants of an historic family.

ARMY AND NAVY MEDAL OF HONOR LEGION
OF THE UNITED STATES OF AMERICA

Objects

Its principles are patriotic allegiance to the United States of America, fidelity to its Constitution and Laws, the security of civil liberty and the preservation of free institutions; to cherish the memories of the valiant deeds in arms for which the Medal of Honor is the insignia; to promote true fellowship among its companions; to advance the best interests of the soldiers and sailors of the United States of America; to extend all possible relief to its needy companions, their widows and children and to stimulate patriotism in the minds of our youth by encouraging the study of the patriotic, military and naval history of our nation.

Membership

The membership of the Legion shall consist of two classes, viz.: 1. Original Companions of the First Class. All persons of good moral character who are, have been or may become soldiers, sailors or marines of the Regular or Volunteer Army, Navy or Marine Corps of the United States of America of whatever rank, who have received or who may hereafter receive a Congress Medal of Honor for distinguished gallantry in battle or for heroism of a specially distinguished character shall be eligible to membership in the Legion.

2. Companions of the Second Class. A son or a daughter, or next of kin by consanguinity or by legal adoption of a Companion of the First Class, who may be nominated by such Companion of the First Class as his successor and holder of his Medal of Honor. The wife or widow and all children of a First Class member shall be eligible to Second Class membership in the Legion.

ARMY AND NAVY UNION OF THE UNITED STATES OF AMERICA

Incorporated March 31, 1888

Objects

To assist in caring for its sick and burying its dead.

Extend a helping hand, pecuniary or otherwise, as may be necessary.

To render such aid as possible to the family or dependents of a deceased comrade or shipmate.

To unite in benevolent and social fellowship those who have served honorably in the Army, Navy or Marine Corps of the United States.

To encourage and aid legislation from Congress and State Legislative bodies beneficial to the welfare of our comrades and the enlisted man of the service.

To defend and elevate the social and material standing of the enlisted men of the United States Army, Navy and Marine Corps and to work for the enactment of laws by State Legislatures, protecting the wearers of the country's uniform against discrimination by theatres or other public places of amusements, and preventing unauthorized people to disgrace the uniform by wearing it in said state.

To perpetuate patriotism and reverence for the Flag, working in a harmonious unit to ever bear to the foremost rank of citizenship the same record of self-sacrifice, unselfishness and the love for humanity and devotion to duty that each member displayed by heroic deeds in the face of the enemies of his country.

To stand for a full measure on the part of all our citizenship and for a like full appreciation on the part of our nation, for all patriotic service and sacrifice, and ultimately to make Fraternity a national anthem, Charity a national virtue, and Loyalty a national hymn.

Membership

The membership of the Army and Navy Union is not limited to any particular war or service, but welcomes all who have served honorably, or are now serving, under that dear old Flag. The organization is governed by the National Corps, composed of the regularly elected officers at the National Encampment held every two years. Local branches in various localities are called Garrisons, which can be organized by any comrade who is eligible to membership. Application fee is not less than $1.00; quarterly dues, 75c, or $3.00 per year. For the convenience of comrades desirous of joining the Army and Navy Union, but who do not live near an established Garrison, there is a Department of Members at Large, governed by the National Corps. The local Garrisons and state departments, composed of Garrisons in any one state, being governed by the department officers or Garrison officers, who are regularly elected every year. Such departments and garrisons being under the supervision of the National Corps to whom they make regular reports.

Members at Large

It makes no difference in what part of the country, insular possessions, or the world you may be residing or stationed, or in what company, organization or naval vessel you may be serving, you can join the Army and Navy Union now as a member at large, and later on can affiliate with a local Garrison when one is formed near you, or should you move to a locality where there is a Garrison.

This department was created for the convenience of officers and enlisted men in active service who are continually moving from place to place, and for comrades and shipmates who reside in remote sections of the country and insular possessions where no local Garrison is organized. The application fee for membership as a member at large is $2.50, which pays for badge, lapel button, certificate of membership, copy of constitution and general laws, and six months dues in advance, the annual dues as a member at large being $1.00. All applications for membership at large must be made to National Headquarters. Address the attached application to the Adjutant General of the Army and Navy Union, advising him of your wishes, and he in turn will forward you an official application blank and an obligation form. These you properly fill out and re-mail to National Headquarters with the fee of $2.50. Should, for any reason, your application not be accepted, the fee will be returned to you.

ARYAN ORDER OF ST. GEORGE OF THE EMPIRE IN AMERICA

Instituted March 11th, 1892

Objects

II.   The purpose of this Society is to promote social virtues, to reprobate fashionable vices and follies, to preserve genealogical records of the families of members and the accounts of their historic greatness as means to further the end by enlivening a feeling of family worth and honor with present memorials.

Membership

V.   Companionship to be conferred must be approved by the Supreme Council, requirements being honorable character, illustrious and honorable family, colonial or noble, of the Aryan race.

X.   The children (male) of the members are to succeed them in membership, according to the prerogative of members of a body corporate to choose their successors.

XII.   All descendants, male, of the first ancestor entitled to membership in the Order, who bear the family name, are eligible as members, and constitute but one family.   That member of a family who represents the eldest line male ranks as Cacique or Chief of the family in the Order.

XIII.   All members receive letters patent from the Order, the Caciques, in addition, transmit to their heirs the titles and decorations of the Order—the imperial two-headed eagle, argent, on whose breast is the red cross of St. George, which is the insignia or coat-of-arms of the Order.

XIV.   Families in the Order are distinguished by emblazoning their coat-of-arms on the two-headed eagle, while the Caciques, bear, in addition, an ancient ducal coronet between the eagle's heads.   The pedigrees of all members are to be lodged with the Grand Recorder, giving recorded ancestral titles and arms with historic evidence.

XV.   That membership in the Order must be restricted to those descended from the following:

1. Those ennobled, knighted, or decorated by royalty for meritorious service.

2. Officers, civil or military, acting under Royal commission (or their male descendants), settled in America from the earliest to latest date. (This includes the whole body of the American colonial magistracy and officers.)

3. Families of honorable mention entitled to coat-of-arms.

ASSOCIATION OF MILITARY SURGEONS OF THE UNITED STATES

Object

The object of the Association shall be to increase the efficiency of the Medical Services of the Army the Navy, the Public Health Service, and of the Organized Militia of the different States by mutual association and the consideration of matters pertaining to the medico-military service of the United States, both in peace and in war.

AZTEC CLUB OF 1847

Founded October 13th, 1847

Objects

This Association, formed and founded in the City of Mexico, in the year 1847, by officers of the United States Army, shall be continued in perpetuity as the "Aztec Club of 1847" with a view to cherish the memories and keep alive the traditions that cluster about the names of those officers who took part in the Mexican War of 1846, '47 and '48.

Membership

The classes of membership shall be three:—Primary, Representative and Associate.

The basis of Primary Membership being personal service as an officer of the Army, Navy or Marine Corps in some part of Mexico during the war with that country in 1846, '47 and '48, the Roll of Members to be "continued in perpetuity" under this constitution shall consist:

First, Of those officers who inaugurated the Aztec Club in the City of Mexico on the 13th of October, 1847, numbering

160 members, and the two honorary members named in Articles I and IV of the Constitution published in March, 1848; and

Second. Of those officers who by resolution of 1871 became eligible to membership since that date, having served in some part of Mexico during the war with that country, and who have been and may hereafter be duly elected members. The names of members admitted on personal application will be enrolled as Primary Members in a list (Number One) to be arranged permanently, in numerical series, in the order of date of admittance—not to be altered except by future additions or by dismissals for cause.

Third. To extend to the memory of comrades killed in battle in Mexico or who died of wounds received in Mexico prior to the formation of our club, all the honorable distinction pertaining to membership in the club, it was resolved in 1883 that upon application by the eldest son or nearest male lineal descendant of the officer so killed such son or nearest male lineal descendant may be eligible to membership as representing his dead relative. When such representative has been duly elected and qualified, the name of the dead officer and the battle where he was killed shall be entered on List Number One, in a separate group with his representative in the order of election.

Fourth. As provided in 1887, the son or nearest male blood relative of any deceased officer who never himself applied for membership (though eligible thereto because of personal service in Mexico during the war) may make written application for admission as the representative of his father or blood relative upon nomination by two members to whom he is known. If elected and qualified, the name of such dead officer shall also be enrolled on List Number One, in the same numerical series, in a separate group, and in the order of the date of admittance of the lineal descendant.

Future Active Membership

Fifth. To provide for the continuance of the Club in conformity with the resolution of September, 1874, each Primary Member admitted upon personal application may nominate as his successor his son or a male blood relative, who during the life of the Primary shall be known as an Associate Member, and entitled to all the privileges of the Club except that of voting, and upon the death of the Primary shall be entitled as his representative to full membership. Should a Primary die with-

Ancient Heraldic and
Chivalric Order
of Albion

The Order of the
White Crane

Military Order of the
Serpent

Order of Runnemede

PLATE II

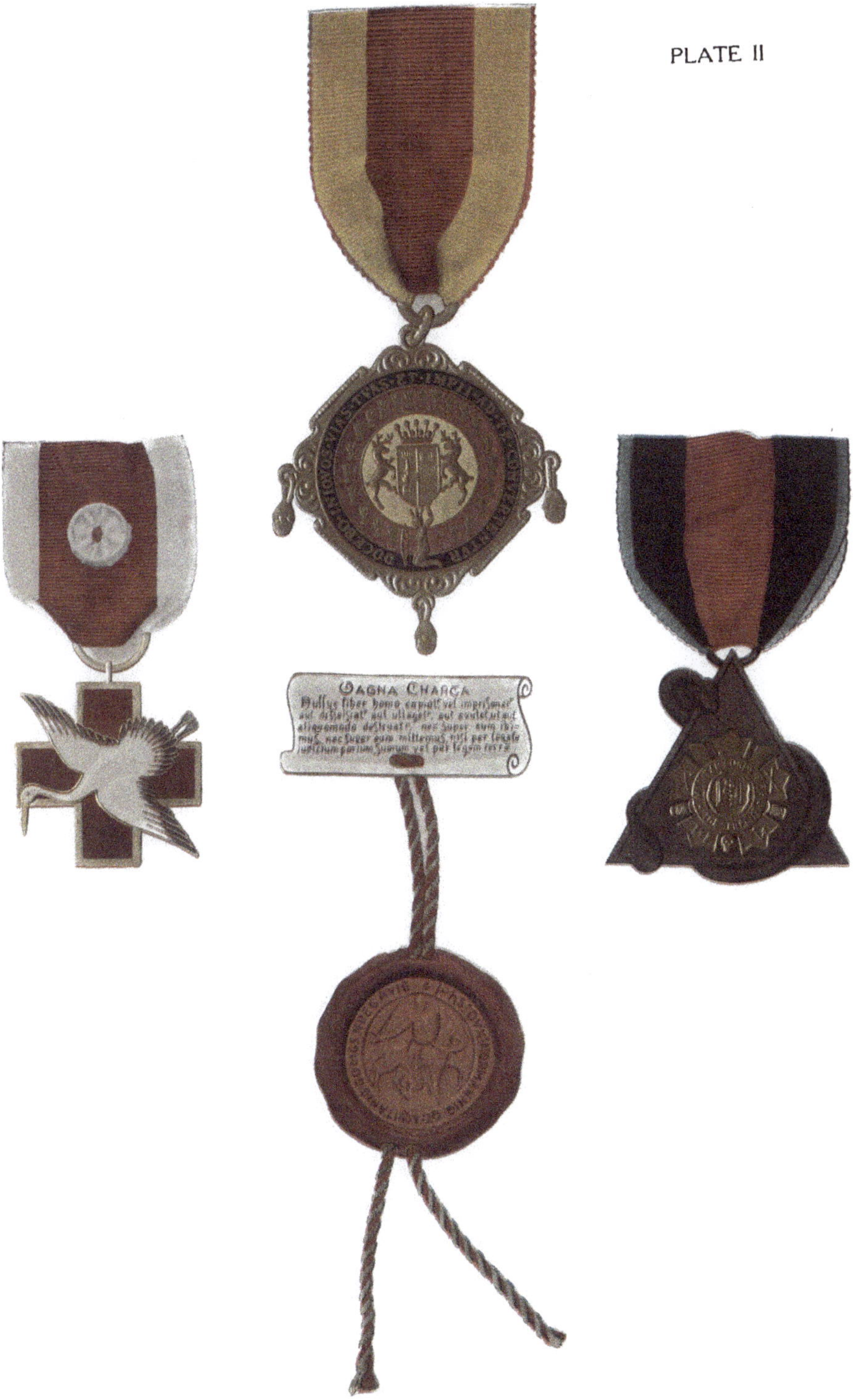

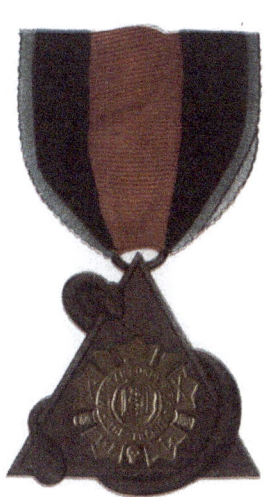

out having named his successor, his son first or nearest blood relative next may, on written application, be nominated as his representative by two members to whom he is known; but no one proposed for an Associate Member or as the representative of a deceased member shall be voted for until the Committee on Admission shall report him eligible and qualified to join the Club.

A Representative Member may nominate as his successor his son or a male blood relative of the Primary Member, whose status shall be that of an Associate Member, as heretofore stated.

If application as the successor of a Primary or Representative Member be made within five years from the date of the death of the Primary or Representative Member, the status of the elected applicant shall be that of Associate Member, in that his initiation fee shall be that of an Associate Member. Such elected applicant shall immediately succeed to full membership as a Successor upon election, and shall be recorded as a Representative Member.

If minors are proposed for membership, their names will be retained for future action until they attain majority.

When the Primary or Representative Member has failed to nominate his successor, then the prospective Representative Member shall be the nearest in blood, male relative of the deceased Primary Member, if there be one qualified to become an acceptable representative of said Primary.

To prevent delay in the admission of candidates to membership in the Club, the Committee on Admissions shall meet four times each year, viz., first Tuesday of January, first Tuesday of April, first Tuesday of June, and first Tuesday of October, and all candidates for admission to the Aztec Club of 1847 who pass the ordeal of that body will be at once reported to the Secretary, who will notify the candidate that he is admitted to membership without further action, provided he duly qualifies for the same.

The Club may act at the regular annual meeting upon any case that may, from any cause, be referred to it.

Should the election of a member take place at the annual meeting of the Club, at least thirteen affirmative votes (in person or by letter) shall be required to admit the applicant, while two negative votes will reject him.

The names of candidates for election shall be presented by members only upon the express request of said candidates.

COLONIAL ORDER OF THE ACORN

Instituted January 30th, 1894, Incorporated February 3d, 1894

Objects

To cherish and perpetuate American traditions and associations, and to promote patriotism and loyalty to our National Institutions.

Membership

It is a pre-requisite to admission that a candidate shall be a descendant, in the male line, of a forefather resident prior to July 4th, 1776, in one of the North American Colonies, that afterwards became the thirteen original States, and shall be nominated for membership and seconded by members of the Order.

COLONIAL SOCIETY OF PENNSYLVANIA

Objects

The object of the Society shall be to celebrate anniversaries of events connected with the settlement of Pennsylvania, which occurred prior to 1700; to collect, preserve, and publish records, documents, printed or in manuscript, relating to the early history of that colony, and to perpetuate the memory of our colonial ancestors.

Membership

Note—Any male person of good character over twenty-one years of age who is lineally descended from a male or female actually settled prior to the year 1700 in any colony of America (now the United States), shall be eligible to membership. But whenever and as long as there shall be three hundred members, no one shall be elected. In all elections to membership, the candidates who are descendants of members shall have precedence.

DAMES OF THE LOYAL LEGION OF THE UNITED STATES

Instituted May 11, 1899

Object

The object of this Order shall be to foster the spirit of Patriotism, and to cherish the memory of those men and women whose distinguished services during the Civil War so largely aided in preserving the integrity of the government of the United States of America.

Membership

Section 1. The members of this Order shall be composed of the wives, mothers, daughters and widows of the companions of the Military Order of the Loyal Legion of the United States, the daughters of the descendants of said companions, who have attained the age of eighteen years, the widows of officers who were not members of the Military Order of the Loyal Legion, but who were eligible as such, the daughters of such deceased officers, and the daughters of the descendants of said officers in lineal descent from the deceased eligible officer.

DAUGHTERS OF THE CINCINNATI

Objects

To renew and foster among its members the friendships formed and cemented amid the trying ordeals of the War of the Revolution, in the Camp, and on the Battlefield, by their ancestors, who by wise leadership and sturdy bravery, achieved the independence of the American Colonies, and established the Government of the United States.

To advance and encourage investigation and study of the history of the Revolution, its causes and results, and to instil in the minds of the rising generations a knowledge of, and reverence for, the intelligent wisdom which planned, and the unconquerable spirit and patient unswerving determination which successfully carried on, the struggle for liberty against overwhelming force and Old World prejudice.

To cherish the memory and record the deeds of the noble women who, with heroic self-abnegation, untiring and unflinching devotion, influenced, encouraged and assisted the Patriot Cause.

To commemorate by celebrations and tablets the achievements of our ancestors in the Revolution, and to gather and carefully preserve documents and relics relating to the Revolutionary period.

To found scholarships for daughters of offiecrs in the regular army or navy of the United States, preferably of Cincinnati ancestry, with a view to self-support.

Qualifications for Membership

1st. Descent from a member of the Society of the Cincinnati, admitted in his own right as an orignal member, in pursuance of the Institution of the Society, as adopted May 13, 1783, at Major-General Baron de Steuben's headquarters at Fishkill-on-the-Hudson, or from an officer of the Revolution who died in the service, and whose offspring were eligible to original membership under such Institution, or from an ancestor who died prior to the formation of the Society and who gave full Revolutionary service.

2d. An invitation from the Society issued by vote of the Board of Managers, upon the application of three members of the Society, to whom the applicant must be favorably and well known.

3d. The applicant must be over the age of eighteen years, and of good moral character.

DAUGHTERS OF THE REVOLUTION

Objects

The objects of this Society shall be to perpetuate the patriotic spirit of the men and women who achieved American Independence; to commemorate prominent events connected with the War of the Revolution; to collect, publish and preserve the rolls, records and historic documents relating to that period; to encourage the study of the country's history; to promote sentiments of friendship and common interest among the members of the Society, and to provide a home for and furnish assistance

Naval Order of the
United States

Veterans
of Foreign Wars of the
United States

The Military Order
of the Loyal Legion
of the United States

The Naval and Military
Order of the
Spanish-American War

Aztec Club of 1847

PLATE III

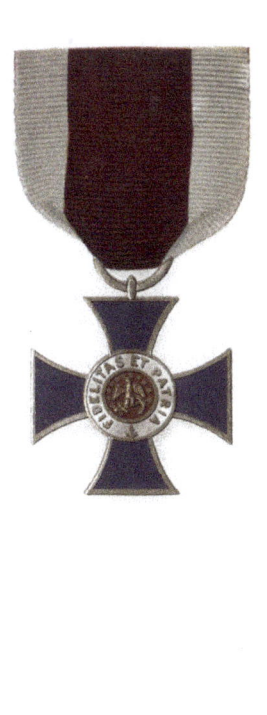

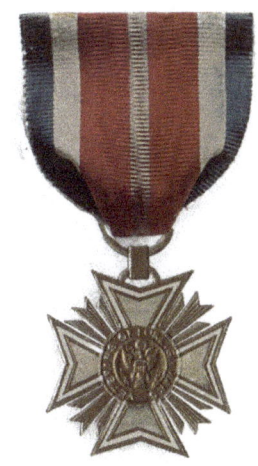

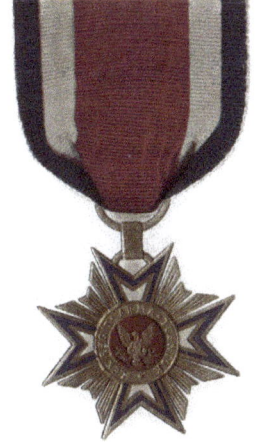

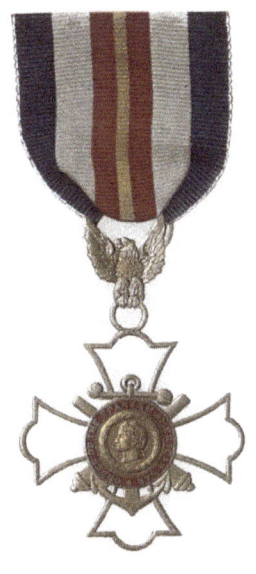

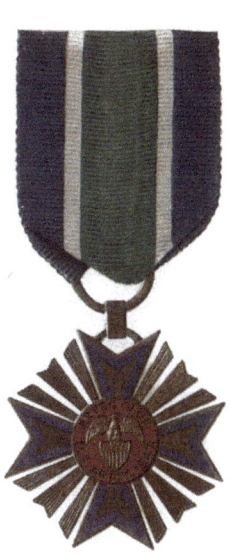

to such Daughters of the Revolution as may be impoverished, when it is in its power to do so.

Membership

Section 1. Qualifications. Any woman shall be eligible to membership in the Daughters of the Revolution who is above the age of 18 years, of good character, and a lineal descendant of an ancestor who

(1) was a signer of the Declaration of Independence, a member of the Continental Congress, or a member of the Congress, Legislature or General Court of any of the Colonies or States; or (2) rendered civil, military or naval service under the authority of any of the Thirteen Colonies or of the Continental Congress; or (3) by service rendered during the War of the Revolution became liable to the penalty of treason against the government of Great Britain; provided that such ancestor always remained loyal to the cause of American Independence.

DESCENDANTS OF THE PIONEERS OF AMERICA— 17TH CENTURY

Organized 1893

Objects

To collect information respecting the history of the families of the first settlers in this country, and to preserve their genealogies.

Membership

Eligibility to membership is derived only through the direct male line, and from one who settled in any part of America prior to the year 1700. This shall include all nationalities.

Members must be at least twenty-one years of age, of good repute and standing in society.

The application for membership must be in writing, and set forth in detail the direct lineage from the original ancestor who emigrated to this country, with the date and place of settlement and from what country he came.

DESCENDANTS OF THE SIGNERS OF THE
DECLARATION OF INDEPENDENCE

Object

The object of the Society shall be to inspire and cultivate a spirit of unselfish patriotism by perpetuating the memory of the Signers of the Declaration of Independence, who in the birth-throes of the Republic mutually pledged their lives, their fortunes and their sacred honor in the cause of liberty.

Membership

All persons over twenty-one years of age who are lineally descended from one of the fifty-six signers of the Declaration of Independence are eligible to membership in the Society. They shall pay an enrollment fee and annual dues and comply with all other conditions of the Constitution and By-Laws.

Children eligible by descent may be enrolled as Junior members upon application of an adult member of the Society and payment of enrollment fee. Upon attaining their majority, Junior members may become full members upon application to and approval of the Board of Governors and payment of annual dues for the current year.

GENERAL SOCIETY OF THE WAR OF 1812

Organized September 14, 1814
Reorganized January 5, 1854

Objects

Whereas, In the Providence of God, victory having crowned the forces of the United States of America in upholding the principles of the Nation against Great Britain in the conflict known as the War of 1812; we, the survivors and descendants of those who participated in that contest, have joined together to perpetuate its memories and victories; to collect and secure for preservation, rolls, records, books and other documents relating to that period; to encourage research and publication of historical data, including memorials of patriots of that era in our National history; to care for and, when necessary, assist in burying actual veterans of that struggle; to cherish, maintain and extend the institutions of American freedom, and foster true patriotism and love of country.

Membership

Any male person above the age of twenty-one (21) years, who participated in, or who is a lineal descendant of one who served during the War of 1812, in the army, navy, revenue-marine, or privateer service of the United States, offering proof thereof satisfactory to the State Society to which he may make application for membership, and who is of good moral character and reputation, may become a member of this Society when approved of by said State Society, under such regulations as it may make for passing upon applications for membership.

In case of the failure of lineal descendants of an actual participant in the War on behalf of the United States, one collateral descendant, who is deemed worthy, may be admitted to represent the said participant.

Provided, always, That such representation shall be limited to the descendant of either a brother or sister of the participant in the War, in right of whose services application for membership is made.

Every application for membership shall be made in writing, upon such form as may be set forth by this Society for that purpose, which application shall be made in duplicate, and one copy thereof filed in the archives of the General Society.

A member in good standing may file one or more supplemental applications, based upon the services in the War of 1812 of either his direct ancestor or of one collateral, who failed to leave lineal descendants, which supplemental application shall be balloted upon in the same manner and with the same effect as upon original applications.

No State Society shall elect to membership persons resident within the territory of another State Society, except upon the written consent given in advance by the Board of Directors of the latter Society. But members changing residence from one State to another, or coming within the jurisdiction of a new State Society, may, at their option, retain membership in the State Society in which they were originally admitted or to which they may have been transferred.

A member of any State Society may be admitted to membership by action of the Board of Directors of another State

Society within the bounds of which he is resident, upon satisfactory proof of his membership and good standing in the Society from which he comes and subject to the rules and regulations of the Society he enters; and thereupon his membership in the first Society shall terminate.

An initiation fee shall not be twice required.

GRAND ARMY OF THE REPUBLIC

Organized March, 1866.　First Post April 6th, 1866

Objects

1.　To preserve and strengthen those kind and fraternal feelings which bind together the soldiers, sailors and marines who united to suppress the late Rebellion, and to perpetuate the memory and history of the dead.

2.　To assist such former comrades in arms as need help and protection, and to extend needful aid to the widows and orphans of those who have fallen.

3.　To maintain true allegiance to the United States of America, based upon a paramount respect for, and fidelity to, its Constitution and Laws; to discountenance whatever tends to weaken loyalty, incites to insurrection, treason, or rebellion, or in any manner impairs the efficiency and permanency of our free institutions; and to encourage the spread of universal liberty, equal rights, and justice to all men.

Membership

Soldiers and sailors of the United States Army, Navy, or Marine Corps, who served between April 12th, 1861, and April 9th, 1865, in the war for the suppression of the Rebellion, and those having been honorably discharged therefrom after such service, and of such State regiments as were called into active service and subject to the orders of U. S. General Officers, between the dates mentioned, shall be eligible to membership in the Grand Army of the Republic.　No person shall be eligible to membership who has at any time borne arms against the United States.

IMPERIAL ORDER OF THE DRAGON
Commemorating the China Relief Expedition of 1900
Membership

Every soldier, sailor or marine at present in the service, or honorably discharged, or retired from the service of the United States Army, Navy or Marine Corps, who is entitled to the Chinese Campaign Medal, may become life members upon the payment of $3.00.

This fee includes the official insignia and life membership card, and no other dues or assessments are to be made.

IMPERIAL ORDER OF THE YELLOW ROSE
History

Prior to 1805 an order of chivarly was formed in America, known as the Imperial Military Order of the Yellow Rose, and on the scroll of the Order the following names are stated to have been found: "Viscount de Fronsac, John Millidge, Augusta, Ga., late Governor; John Irvine Bulloch, Judge Archibald Stobo Bulloch, of Savannah, Ga.; Noble Wymberley Jones, M. D.; John Glen, Chief Justice of Georgia; Major John Habersham, W. Harden and J. Maxwell, all of Georgia, and James De Veaux and John Rutledge, of South Carolina."

This Order was revised May 11, 1908, in Washington City, D. C., by Dr. Joseph Gaston Baillie Bulloch, grandson of John Irvine Bulloch, and great-grandson of Judge John Glen and also descended from Dr. Noble Wymberley Jones, the title of Military being left off, and the proviso added that "none but those of Royal descent shall hereafter be admitted into membership in the Order." After several meetings and consultations a constitution was adopted and application for a charter was made which was granted under the laws of the United States in the District of Columbia on the 15th of June, 1908.

Object

To keep an authentic record of the ancestry of its members, to further historical research and genealogical purposes.

Membership

All those, male and female, of Royal lineage of Aryan race in any part of the world.

MILITARY ORDER OF FOREIGN WARS OF THE UNITED STATES

Objects

Whereas, Pursuant to the original Institution of the Order, the Military Order of Foreign Wars of the United States—National Commandery has, by the officers of the said several State Commanderies in meeting duly assembled, been instituted to honor and perpetuate the names of brave and loyal men; to keep in mind the memory of their martial deeds and the victories which they helped to gain; to strengthen the ties of fellowship among the Companions of the Order; to foster the cultivation of Military and Naval Science; and to aid in maintaining National Honor, Union and Independence;

Companionship

Section 1. Any male person, above the age of twenty-one years, a citizen of the United States, of good moral character and reputation, shall be eligible to Companionship in this Order upon further qualifying as hereinafter provided. When duly admitted such persons shall be known as "Companions." These shall be either "Veteran Companions," "Hereditary Companions" or "Honorary Companions."

Section 2. Veteran Companions—These shall be persons who performed active Military or Naval duty in any of the wars designated in Section IV of this Article, as commissioned officers therein, of the Regular or Volunteer Army and Navy or Militia, the Navy or Marine Corps, and who received their commissions by direct act of either Federal or State authority,

Provided, That when the claim of eligibility is based upon the service of was honorably discharged therefrom, and

Provided, That where the commission was received from one of the States, it must be satisfactorily shown, that the Officer was actually called into service by State or National Authority for the purpose of the designated War.

Section 3. Hereditary Companions—These shall be the direct male lineal descendants, in the male line, of any Veteran Companion; or of a commissioned officer, as the Propositus, who performed active military or naval duty, as a commissioned officer, in any of said wars, and who received his commission by direct act of one of the thirteen original Colonies, or of Vermont, or of the Continental Congress, or of one of the States, or of the United States.

26

Provided, That such Propositus remained always loyal to his cause and was either killed or died in service or was honorably discharged therefrom; and

Provided, That when the claim to eligibility is based upon the service of an ancestor in the "Militia" it must be satisfactorily shown that such ancestor was actually called into the service of one of said thirteen original Colonies, or of Vermont, or of the Continental Congress, or of one of the States, or of the United States, and performed military duty; and

Provided, That when the claim to eligibility is based upon the service of an ancestor as a "Naval" or "Marine" officer, it must be satisfactorily shown that such service was regularly performed in the Continental Navy or in the Navy of one of the thirteen original Colonies, or of Vermont, or of one of the States, or of the United States or an armed vessel, other than a merchant ship, which sailed under letters of marque and reprisal, and that such ancestor was duly enrolled in the ship's company as a commissioned officer.

Section 4.   Such service must be satisfactorily shown to have been performed in one of the following wars:

The War of the Revolution, between the 19th day of April, 1775, and the 19th day of April, 1783;

The War with Tripoli, between the 10th day of June, 1801, and the 4th day of June, 1805;

The War of 1812, between the 18th day of June, 1812, and the 18th day of February, 1815;

The Mexican War, between the 9th day of May, 1846, and the 4th day of July, 1848;

The War with Spain, between the 21st day of April, 1898, and the 11th day of April, 1899, and

The China Relief Expedition, between the 20th day of June, 1900, and the 12th day of May, 1901.

That all men who served as commissioned officers in all future wars with Foreign Powers, which are recognized or pronounced to be wars by the United States Government, shall be eligible to this Order.

Section 5.   No applicant shall be admitted to Companionship in this Order who is not judged to be worthy of becoming a Companion and supporter thereof.

Section 6.   Honorary Companionship—The President of the United States; ex-Presidents of the United States; General

Officers of the Army of the United States, not below the rank of Major-General; Flag Officers of the Navy of the United States, not below the rank of Rear-Admiral; shall alone be eligible to Honorary Companionship in this Order, and when admitted shall be known as "Honorary Companions."

MILITARY ORDER OF MORO CAMPAIGNS

Objects

The aim of the Military Order of Moro Campaigns is to record a complete history of the service of each organization in Mindanao and the Jolo Archipelago since the American occupation, May 18, 1899, including therein the history of each individual, so far as is practicable.

Membership

Any person who took part in the expeditions against the Moros between July 15, 1903, and December 31st, 1904.

MILITARY ORDER OF CARABAO

Objects

Whereas, In the Providence of God, the forces of the United States of America having been drawn to the Philippine Islands in the conflict known as "The Spanish-American War of 1898," and the subsequent insurrection against the United States in the Philippine Islands, we, the survivors and descendants of those who participated in that contest, have joined together to foster a high standard of military and social duty; to perpetuate the memory of military services in the Philippines; to strengthen the ties of fellowship; to collect and secure for preservation rolls, records, relics, books and other documents relating to that period; to encourage research and publication of historical data, and to cherish, maintain and extend the institutions of American freedom.

Membership

Section 1. Any person who shall have honorably served in the Philippine Islands between May 1, 1898, and July 4, 1902, both dates inclusive, as a commissioned officer of the

The Veteran Corps
of Artillery of the
State of New York

General Society of the
War of 1812

National Society of
Patriotic Women
of America

The Order of the
Founders and Patriots
of America

PLATE IV

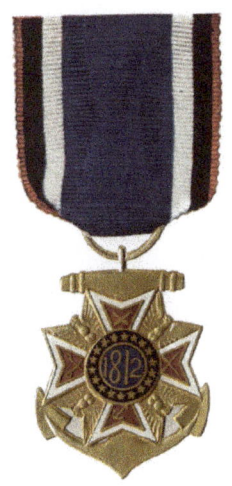

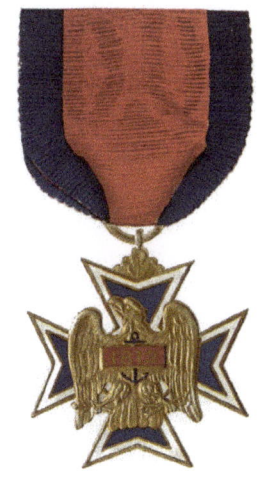

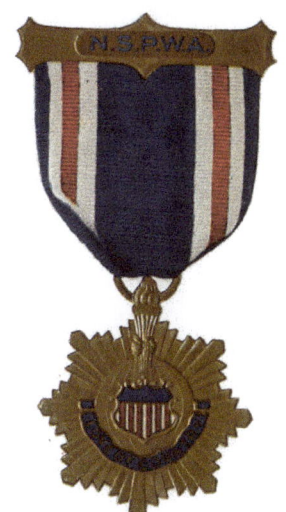

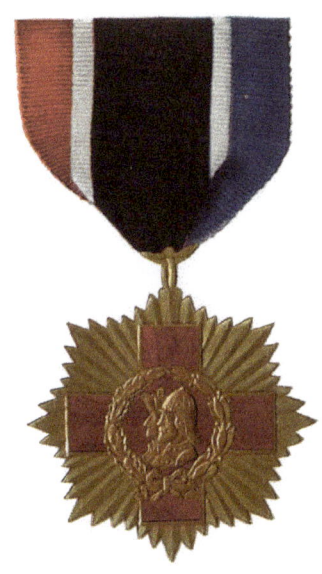

United States Regular or Volunteer Army, Navy, Marine Corps, Philippine Scouts, or as a Naval Cadet or Midshipman, or as Acting Assistant Surgeon, Contract Surgeon, Contract Dental Surgeon, or any person who so served as an enlisted man in the United States Army, Navy or Marine Corps and subsequently received a commission for appointment in any of the above-named classes, shall be eligible for election as a Veteran Carabao; and any accredited war correspondent who served in the Philippine Islands between May 1, 1898, and July 4, 1902, both dates inclusive, shall be eligible to election as an Associate Carabao, with all the privileges of Carabaos, except those of voting and holding office.

Section 2. Honorary membership in the Order may be conferred by the Main Corral upon the President of the United States and upon the Governor-Generals of the Philippines or upon those who have held that office.

Section 3. The oldest lineal male descendant over 21 years of age of a Veteran Carabao or person eligible to become one shall be eligible to join the Order as a Tenero during his ancestor's life, and at his death the Tenero shall become a Hereditary Carabao.

MILITARY ORDER OF THE DRAGON

Objects

The purpose of the Order shall be to record the history and conserve the memory of the military campaign in China in the year 1900.

Membership

The membership of the Order shall consist of four classes:

Active Members. All regular and volunteer commissioned officers of the United States Army, Navy and Marine Corps, Acting Assistant Surgeons and authorized Volunteer Staff Officers, who served as such, or as an enlisted man, in North China or in the Gulf of Pechili in connection with or as a part of any military operation and under the orders of the respective Army and Navy Commanders thereof between June 15th and December 31st, 1900, and all members of the Diplomatic and Consular services of the United States in Tientsin and Peking during said period shall be eligible as active members.

Hereditary Members. The nearest male descendant, 21 years of age or over, of active members, may become hereditary members upon election by the Executive Committee and the payment of the fees and dues hereinafter provided. Hereditary members shall not be entitled to vote or hold office. Upon the death of the active member from whom the hereditary member derives eligibility, such hereditary member shall become an active member by hereditary, and shall be transferred to the active list, with all its rights and privileges.

Honorary Members. All members of the foreign diplomatic corps present on duty in Peking at any time during the period from June 15th to December 31st, 1900, all military and naval commissioned officers of other services than that of the United States present in North China, or in the Gulf of Pechili, and engaged in the military operations thereat, between the dates above specified, may become Honorary Members upon application.

Honorary Hereditary Members. Male descendants of 21 years of age or over, of those eligible to Honorary Membership, may become Honorary Hereditary Members upon election by the Executive Committee.

MILITARY ORDER OF THE FRENCH ALLIANCE
Object

To carry out the injunctions of Washington in his farewell address to the American people.

"The Unity of Government, which constitutes you one people, . . . is a main pillar in the edifice of your real independence. . . . The name of American, which belongs to you in your national capacity, must always exalt the just pride of patriotism more than any appellation derived from local discriminations. . . . . In contemplating the causes which may disturb our Union, it occurs as matter of serious concern that any ground should have been furnished for characterizing parties by geographical discrimination—Northern and Southern, Atlantic and Western. . . . To the efficacy and permanency of your Union, a government for the whole is indispensable. . . . The basis of our political system is the right of the people to make and to alter their constitution of government; but the constitution which at any time exists, until changed by an explicit and authentic act of the whole people, is sacredly obligatory upon all. . . . Resist with care the spirit of innovation upon its principles. . . . Let me warn you in the most solemn manner against the baneful effects of the spirit of party. . . The habits of thinking in a free country should inspire caution in those intrusted with its administration, to confine themselves within their respective constitutional spheres, avoiding in the exercise of the powers of one department to encroach upon another. . . . If, in the opinion of the people, the distribution or modification of the constitutional powers be in any particular wrong, let it be corrected by an amendment in the way which the constitution designates; but let there be no change by usurpation. . . . Of all the dispositions and habits which lead to political prosperity, religion and morality are indispensable supports. . . . Promote, as an object of primary importance, institutions for the general diffusion of knowledge. . . . As a very important source of strength and security, cherish public credit. . . . Observe good faith and justice towards all nations; cultivate peace and harmony with all. . . . Inveterate antipathies against particular nations and passionate attachments for others should be excluded. . . . Against the insidious wiles of foreign influence, the jealousy of a free people ought to be constantly awake. . . . The great rule of conduct for us in regard to foreign nations is, in extending our commercial relations, to have with them as little political connection as possible. . . . Taking care always to keep ourselves, by suitable establishment, on a respectable defensive posture, we may safely trust to temporary alliances for extraordinary emergencies. . . . The duty of holding a neutral conduct (in case of war between foreign nations) may be inferred from the obligation which justice and humanity impose on every nation, in cases in which it is free to act, to maintain inviolate the relations of peace and amity towards other nations."

Membership

Lineal male descendants through officers of the colonists and our French Allies, of the Revolutionary Army and Navy who took part in the Revolutionary War against the British.

MILITARY ORDER OF THE MIDNIGHT SUN

Information as to Objects and Requirements for Membership not available at time of publication.

MILITARY ORDER OF THE SERPENT

Founded January 1st, 1904.   Incorporated August 6th, 1907

Objects

To maintain a secret and social Society to perpetuate the memories of the war with Spain, the incident struggle in the Philippines, the China Relief Expedition; for literary purposes connected with these wars, as well as to more firmly establish good fellowship among the comrades of the United Spanish War Veterans.

Membership

Is limited to members of the United Spanish War Veterans, in good standing in that body.

NATIONAL ASSOCIATION OF NAVAL VETERANS, U. S. OF A., 1861-1865

Organized January 13th, 1887

Membership

Limited to officers and men who served in the United States Navy from 1861 to 1865.

NATIONAL SOCIETY AMERICANS OF ROYAL DESCENT

Incorporated May 2d, 1908

Object

The Society was formed for the purpose of preserving the historical ancestry of the early settlers of America.

Membership

The Society is composed of both men and women of good standing in one of the American Ancestral Societies other than

Aryan Order of
Saint George of the
Empire in America

Descendants of
the Signers of the
Declaration
of Independence

Society of the Daughters
of Holland Dames

Military Order of the
Dragon

PLATE V

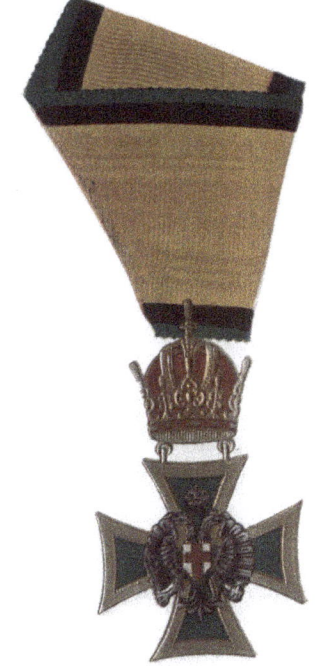

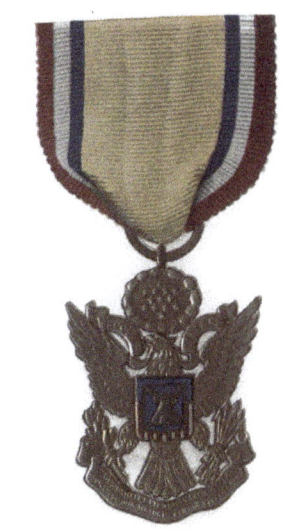

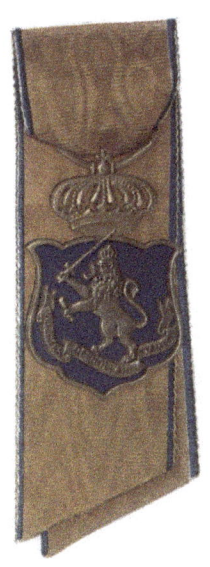

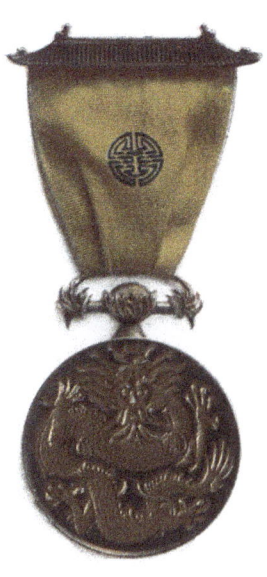

the Daughters of the American Revolution, and of "Royal Descent." Every application for membership shall be accompanied by proof of eligibility. The payment of thirty dollars shall constitute life membership and exemption from assessment. This payment shall accompany the candidate's application papers, which have to be endorsed by an officer of a Colonial Society. In the event that a candidate for membership is not found eligible, the membership fee paid shall be refunded, less a charge of twenty dollars for genealogical examination.

NATIONAL SOCIETY COLONIAL DAMES
XVII CENTURY

Organized July 24, 1915, following Meeting of the International Genealogical Congress at San Francisco

Objects

To aid in establishing a College of Heraldry in America; to establish chairs of historical research in state universities; to commemorate the deeds of the men and women of the Colonial period.

Membership

By invitation. Life membership, $10. Certificate descending to next of kin without further dues.

NATIONAL SOCIETY COLONIAL DAUGHTERS
OF AMERICA

Organized May 13th, 1907

Object

To perpetuate the memory of the women of the Colonial period from 1607 to 1776—the noble women who established homes, founded families, introduced refinement and culture and made civilization and sound morals permanent occupants of our country.

Membership

Any gentlewoman who has attained her sixteenth year, of good moral character and standing, who is acceptable to the Society, is eligible to membership in the Society of Colonial Daughters, who is descended from an ancestor who served in any of the battles under Colonial authority, or who filled the office of Governor, Deputy Governor, Lieutenant Governor, member of the Council or Assembly or delegate to the Legislature, or as a military, naval or marine officer in the service of the colonies, or under the banner of Great Britain in North America, in the wars in which said colonies participated or furnished troops from the settlement of Virginia in 1607 to the battle of Lexington 1775, and descendants and members of Committee of Safety 1775-1776, members of Continental Congresses 1774-1775 and Signers of Declaration of Independence.

NATIONAL SOCIETY OF DAUGHTERS OF FOUNDERS AND PATRIOTS OF AMERICA

Objects

Section 1. To associate congenial women whose ancestors struggled together for life, liberty, home and happiness in this land when it was a new and unknown country, and whose lines of descent come through patriots who sustained the Colonies in the struggle for independence in the Revolutionary War.

Section 2. To teach reverent regard for the names and history, character, deeds and heroism of the founders of this country and their patriotic descendants and to inculcate patriotism in the present and succeeding generations.

Section 3. To discover and preserve family records and history otherwise unwritten and unknown, of the first Colonists, their ancestors and descendants.

Section 4. To commemorate events of the history of the Colonies and of the Republic, and in times of war to obtain and forward supplies for field hospitals.

Membership

Section 1. Eligibility for membership is founded upon descent from patriotic ancestry in unbroken line through the Colonial times and the Revolutionary War.

Section 2. Any woman, above the age of eighteen years, of good moral character and reputation, is eligible to membership, provided that she is descended in the direct paternal line of either father or mother from an ancestor who settled in any of the Colonies now included in the United States of America, from the settlement of Jamestown, Va., May 13, 1607, to May 13, 1687, and provided that during the Revolutionary War, an ancestor in said direct line, by personal service in a civil or military capacity, assisted in establishing American Independence.

NATIONAL SOCIETY OF NEW ENGLAND WOMEN

Instituted January 24th, 1895. Incorporated March 4th, 1895

Objects

To promote social and intellectual intercourse among its members and to offer advice and asistance to women of New England birth and ancestry, residing in portions of the United States other than New England.

It is not the intention to make this a benevolent society. It is only intended to render a service in any way to any New England women who may need it. The intention of the Society is to carry out New England principles as far as possible, of advancing the cause of intellectual progress, of searching up new ideas and introducing anything of a social nature which would seem to add to the happiness of its members.

Membership

(a). Any woman of American parentage over eighteen years of age, who was born in New England and both of whose parents were born in New England, is eligible for membership in this Society.

(b). If not of New England birth, she must represent through both parents at least two generations of New England ancestry, or she must represent through one parent at least three generations of New England ancestry.

(c). New England birth on the part of an applicant shall count as one generation.

(d). An applicant descended from a pioneer, who became a permanent settler in New England prior to 1645, shall have the privilege of representing through said pioneer one generation.

NATIONAL SOCIETY OF PATRIOTIC WOMEN OF AMERICA

Objects

1. To foster love of country.

2. To encourage fitting celebrations of patriotic anniversaries.

3. To teach immigrants, and especially their children, the true meaning of the American Flag, and what it stands for, in order that they may become loyal citizens of our Republic.

4. To make this Society an active factor in patriotic educational progress.

5. To extend the work of this Society by forming branch societies in other cities and states of the Union.

Membership

Any woman is eligible for membership who will subscribe to the objects of this Society, subject to the rules for admission set forth in the By-Laws.

NATIONAL SOCIETY OF THE ARMY OF THE PHILIPPINES

Any officer, soldier or sailor of the regular or volunteer Army, Navy and Marine Corps who served honorably in the Philippine Islands during the Spanish-American War or in the Philippine insurrection, including Jolo and Mindanao expeditions of 1906, is eligible to membership.

NATIONAL SOCIETY OF THE CHILDREN OF THE AMERICAN REVOLUTION

Incorporated April 11th, 1895

Objects

We, the children and youth of America, in order to know more about our country from its formation and thus grow up into good citizens, with a love for, and an understanding of, the principles and institutions of our ancestors, do unite under

The Huguenot Society
of America

The Society of the
Army of the Potomac

The American
Red Cross

The Hereditary Order
of Descendants of
Colonial Governors
Prior to 1750

PLATE VI

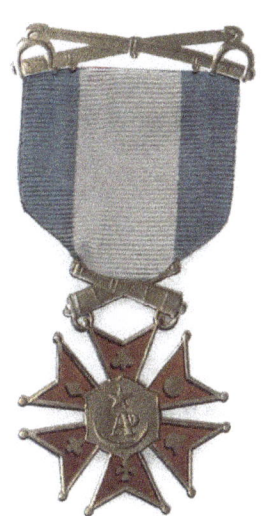
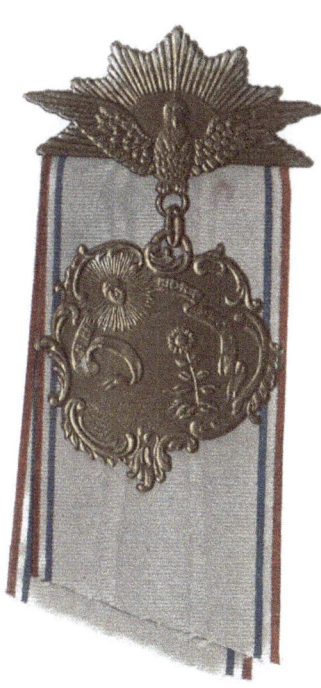
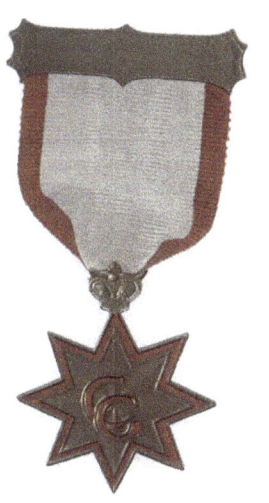
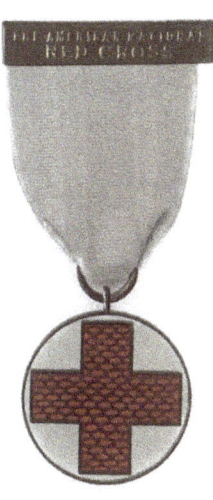

the guidance and government of the Daughters of the American Revolution, in the Society to be called the National Society of the Children of the American Revolution.

We take as objects of this Society, to work for: First, the acquisition of knowledge of American history, so that we may understand and love our country better, and then any patriotic work that will help us to that end, keeping a constant endeavor to influence all other children and youth to the same purpose; to help to save the places made sacred by the American men and women who forwarded American Independence; to find out and to honor the lives of children and youth of the Colonies and of the American Revolution; to promote the celebration of all patriotic anniversaries; to place a copy of the Declaration of Independence and other historic documents in every place appropriate for them; to hold our American flag sacred above every other flag on earth. In short, to follow the injunctions of Washington, who, in his youth, served his country, till we can perform the duties of good citizens.

And to love, uphold, and extend the institutions of American liberty and patriotism, and the principles that made and saved our country.

Membership

All children and youth of America, of both sexes, from birth to the age of eighteen years for the girls and twenty-one years for the boys, may join this Society, provided they descend in direct line from patriotic ancestors who helped to plant or to perpetuate this country in the Revolutionary War.

One of the reasons for starting this work is that it will tend to popularize the work of the public school toward patriotism and good government.

Those children who are not eligible for membership are to be gathered by the Local Societies into all its public meetings, into its plans, and its work, and its pleasures; so that the movement may be said to be one of the broadest and most beneficent that has touched child life.

NATIONAL SOCIETY UNITED STATES DAUGHTERS OF 1812

Organized January 8th, 1892
Incorporated by Act of Congress February 25th, 1901

Purpose

Section 1.   In general, our one purpose is the promotion of patriotism, and we seek to carry out the patriotic, historical, educational and benevolent purposes stated in our charter.

In particular, we strive to preserve and increase knowledge of the history of the American people, by the preservation of documents and relics, the marking of historic spots, the recording of family histories and traditions, the celebrating of patriotic anniversaries, and especially the emphasizing and teaching of heroic deeds in the civil, military and naval life of those who moulded this government of the United States, and saved it from foes both within and without, between the close of the American Revolution, and the close of the War of 1812.

Sec. 2.   We urge the United States Government, through an Act of Congress, to compile and publish authentic records of men in military, naval and civil service from 1784 to 1815, inclusive.

Sec. 3.   We make it the duty of each state society to acquire if possible and to preserve documents and records of events for which its state is renowned, and to advise the historian national of such possessions and of any unpublished historical data concerning the state during this period.

Membership

Any white woman over eighteen years of age, of good character, who offers satisfactory proof that she is a lineal descendant of an ancestor who rendered civil, military or naval service to his country during the years 1784-1815, inclusive, is eligible to membership, provided the applicant be acceptable to the society.

Civil service must have been in some one of the following capacities:

> A member of the Continental, or United States Congresses.
> A member of the legislature of one of the first eighteen States.

A delegate to the convention which framed the Constitution of the United States.

A member of a state convention which ratified said Constitution.

An elector of one of the first four presidents of the United States.

A legislative, executive or judicial officer of the United States (not state) Government, including such appointive national officers as treaty commissioner, etc.

Military or naval service may have been in any one of the following insurrections or wars:

Wyoming Valley, Pennsylvania, 1784-87.

Shay's Rebellion, Massachusetts, 1786-87.

Wars with the Indians, 1784-1815.

Whiskey Insurrection, Pennsylvania, 1794.

War with France (Undeclared), 1798-1800.

Sabine Expedition, Louisiana, 1806.

Attack of British warship Leopard upon United States frigate Chesapeake, 1807.

Embargo Troubles in Lake Champlain, 1808.

Engagement between United States frigate "President" and British ship "Little Belt," 1811.

Expedition against Lafitte Pirates, 1814.

War with the Barbary Powers, 1801-05 and 1815.

War with Great Britain, 1812-15. Service in the army or navy, either as officer or as private, or the giving of notable aid to the army or navy.

NAVY LEAGUE OF THE UNITED STATES

Incorporated 1903

Objects

The Navy League believes that most modern wars arise largely from commercial rivalries; that following the present war will come the most drastic commercial readjustment and the most dangerous rivalries ever known; that the United States will be the storm center of these disturbances; and that, consequently, it is our duty to guard ourselves against these dangers while there is yet time.

The first need was more ships and more men to make our country second, at least, among the great naval powers. This need is in process of realization, due largely to the fact that the Navy League has been instrumental in creating an overwhelming public sentiment for naval preparedness and bringing that sentiment to bear upon the constituted authorities.

It is now the purpose of the League to endeavor to sustain and keep alive popular interest in the Navy and to drive home the fact that what has been accomplished is only a beginning. The country needs a national defense commission to study international relations and advise the President and Congress as to policies of national defense; it needs the budget system; it needs the utmost efficiency with economy in naval administration; and it needs a great merchant marine to enable our export trade to meet foreign competition and to supply the naval auxiliaries without which in time of war our fleet might be helpless. These are the most important but by no means all, of the questions involved in the building up of a real efficient fighting machine capable of insuring the peace and prosperity of the nation.

Membership

Any American citizen is eligible to become a member of the League.

NAVAL ORDER OF THE UNITED STATES

Organized July 4, 1890

This organization is believed to be the first hereditary society in which eligibility was "dependent on purely naval service."

The Naval Order consists of the General Commandery and State Commanderies. The legislative body for the whole Order is the Congress, which, composed of the General Officers and Delegates from each Commandery, meets in regular session every third year, on October 5th, the anniversary of the Adoption by Congress in 1775 of the resolution formally authorizing the fitting-out of the first ships of the navy.

Objects

Whereas, Many of the principal battles and famous victories of the several wars in which the United States has participated were fought and achieved by the Naval forces;

Whereas, It is well and fitting that the illustrious deeds of the great Naval commanders, their companion officers in arms and their subordinates in the Wars of the United States should be forever honored and respected;

Therefore, Entertaining the most exalted admiration for the undying achievements of the Navy, we, the survivors and descendants of participants of those memorable conflicts, have joined ourselves together and have instituted the "Naval Order of the United States," that we may transmit to our latest posterity their glorious names and memories; and to encourage research and publication of data pertaining to Naval art and science, and to establish libraries in which to preserve all documents, rolls, books, portraits and relics relating to the Navy and its heroes at all times.

Membership

The following shall be eligible to membership: Commissioned officers of the Navy and of the Marine Corps of the United States, whether of the regular or volunteer service, graduates of the Naval Academy, and commissioned officers of the Revenue Marine Service who have served under the orders of the Navy Department in time of war; and all persons who have held any such commission under the authority of any of the thirteen original Colonies or States, or of the Continental Congress, or of the United States. Provided, that those who have left the service shall have resigned with honorable record or shall have been honorably discharged. And provided further, that no one who shall at any time have borne arms against the Government of the United States shall be eligible.

All male descendants over twenty-one years of age of those who are eligible as above, or, in default thereof, one collateral representative.

ORDER OF AMERICANS OF ARMORIAL ANCESTRY

Founded by Mrs. Wm. Gerry Slade
Instituted 1903-4

Objects

This is an Order founded wholly on Heraldic Ancestry, to promote genealogical, biographical and historical research, and to place upon record the ancestry of such of the founders of this country as can be definitely traced into the Mother Country.

It is for men and women who are descended from those who were entitled to bear arms.

Membership

Membership is acquired by invitation and an unbroken and proven line to the bearer of a grant or confirmation of arms, or to one who is recorded as entitled to bear coat-armor. The admission fee constitutes life membership, with no dues, and carries with it the insignia of the Order in gold bearing the arms of the United States and of the first five countries which sent its earliest settlers to America, from which its ancestry is largely derived.

ORDER OF INDIAN WARS OF THE UNITED STATES

Objects

The objects of this Society shall be to perpetuate the memories of the services rendered by the military forces of the United States in their conflicts and wars against hostile Indians within the territory or jurisdiction of the United States, and to collect and secure for publication historical data relating to the instances of heroic service and personal devotion by which Indian warfare has been illustrated.

Membership

Section 1. Companions of this Society shall be elected as herein provided and for the two classes specified, and shall be designated as Original and Hereditary Companions.

Original Companions

Commissioned officers and honorably discharged commissioned officers of the U. S. Army, Navy and Marine Corps, and of State and Territorial Military Organizations, and Acting Assistant Surgeons, U. S. Army, who have been or who hereafter may be engaged in the service of the United States in any military grade whatsoever, in conflicts, battles or actual field service against hostile Indians within the jurisdiction of the United States. Those becoming companions under any of the foregoing qualifications shall be designated as Original Companions.

Hereditary Companions

The male descendants of Original Companions and the male descendants of those eligible for membership as Original Companions, but who died without becoming Companions, such descendants having attained the age of twenty-one years, shall be eligible for membership and shall, when duly elected, be designated as Hereditary Companions.

Commissioned officers of the Army, Navy and Marine Corps of the United States, descendants of honorably discharged enlisted men who had the qualifications requisite for eligibility for membership as Original Companions save that of having been Commissioned, are also eligible, and may be elected as Hereditary Companions.

Section 2. Any Original Companion, or any Hereditary Companion, having no direct male descendant, may, by writing, filed with the Recorder, nominate an Hereditary Companion descending only from his own brother or sister, and the person so nominated shall, upon attaining the age of twenty-one years, be eligible as an Hereditary Companion.

Section 3. No person shall be deemed eligible for membership in the Society who has not maintained a good moral character and reputation.

Section 4. The eligibility of any person to be an Heridi-tary Companion shall not lapse by reason of any person in the line of descent either failing to become a Companion of the Society or forfeiting, for any cause, his membership or eligibility.

ORDER OF RUNNEMEDE

Instituted January 8th, 1898

Objects

To perpetuate the memory of the men, who after many defeats, finally secured the charter of rights and liberties, properly called the Magna Charta, from their sovereign, John, King of England, which he ratified and delivered to them "in the meadow which is called Runnemede, between Windsor and Staines," on the 15th day of June (O. S.) A. D. 1215.

To keep fresh in our minds the events connected with this celebrated episode in the annals of the English race.

To promote good fellowship among the descendants of those who extorted the Magna Charta from King John.

To inspire members of the Order and others, with admiration, and to foster respect, for the principles of Constitutional Government, first established by the statutes of the Great Charter granted by King John.

To celebrate the anniversary of the date (June 15th) of the granting of this the most celebrated charter of rights and liberties.

The Order of Runnemede shall be governed by the following Statutes, to wit:

Membership

The membership of the Order shall be composed of its Founders, and of men qualified under Section 1 of this Statute.

Section 1. Any man shall be eligible to membership in the Order, who has been proposed in writing by a member of the Order, with the written consent of the candidate, and has been recommended for election by two members, one of whom is personally acquainted with him, providing always, that he is a lineal descendant, in the male, or female line, of an ancestor who rendered actual service in, or before, the year A. D. 1215, towards securing the articles of constitutional liberty, known as the Magna Charta, from John, King of England, in the years 1214-1215.

Section 2. The membership of the Order shall be divided into two bodies, called First Class and Second Class.

Section 3. The First Class shall be limited to one hundred members, and shall be composed of (a) the Founders of

44

Society of the Army of
Santiago de Cuba

Military Order of
Foreign Wars of the
United States

The
Pennsylvania-German
Society

Society of the
Porto Rican Expedition

The Society of the
Ark and the Dove

PLATE VII

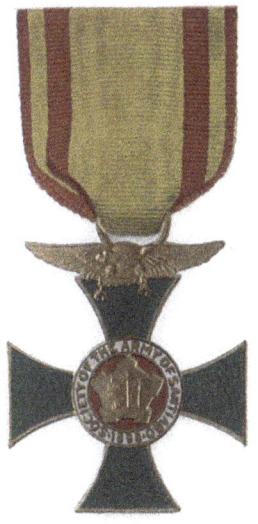

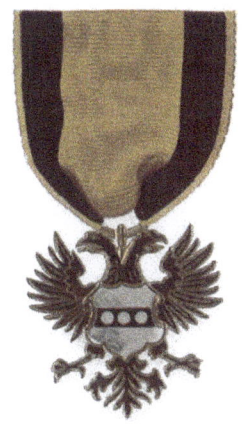

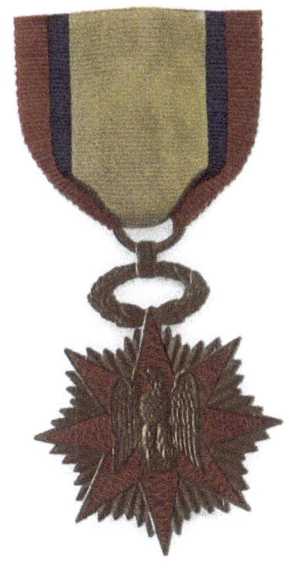

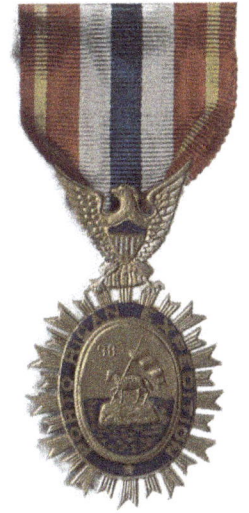

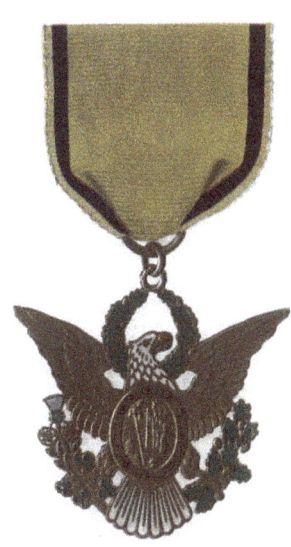

the Order, and of (b) lineal male descendants of one or more of the twenty-five barons who were selected to be the Sureties for the proper observance of the statutes contained in the Magna Charta, namely: William d'Albini, Hugh le Bigod, Roger le Bigod, Henry de Bohun, Gilbert de Clare, Richard de Clare, John Fitz Robert, Robert Fitz Walter, William de Fortibus, William de Hardell, William de Huntingfield, John de Lacie, William de Malet, Geoffrey de Mandeville, William le Marshall, Richard de Montfichet, Roger de Mowbray, William de Mowbray, Richard de Percy, Saher de Quincey, Robert de Roos, Geoffrey de Say, Robert de Vere, Eustace de Vesci, William de Lanvallei.

Section 4.   The Second Class shall be unlimited in its membership, and shall be composed of lineal male descendants of the Sureties for the Magna Charta, or of any men who were unfailing in their loyalty to the cause of the Magna Charta, before or in the year 1215.

Section 5.   To provide for the continuance of the Order.

1.   Each member of the First Class may, in writing, nominate to the Keeper of the Rolls, his successor in membership in that Class, and this possible successor must be qualified, as under Section 3, Paragraph B, of this Statute 1, who, during the lifetime of the primary member, may have active membership of the Order, in the Second Class, and he shall be entitled to any and all the privileges of the Order.   And upon the decease of the primary member who nominated him, he shall be eligible as his representative, to full membership in the First Class, providing always, that he is, in the opinion of the majority of the Court of Eligibility, fit in all other respects, and the same shall so have been certified by it to the Sureties, who shall thereupon notify the candidate of his promotion.

2.   The failure on the part of a person eligible by succession to membership in the First Class, to apply for his promotion within six months after being informed at his last known address by the Keeper of the Rolls, of the existence of his claim, shall be interpreted as a surrender thereof forever by him, and the Keeper of the Rolls must thereupon so notify the Sureties, who may then declare this particular membership in the First Class vacant.

3.   Should a member of the First Class die without having nominated his successor, it must be taken for granted that the deceased desired his membership to lapse, whereupon it is

the duty of the Keeper of the Rolls, to notify the Sureties of a vacancy in the First Class.

4.   Vacancies in the First Class shall be filled by the Sureties only from the membership of the Second Class, after its first complement.

Section 6.   Honorary Membership may be conferred in the First Class only by the majority of the Sureties, at a meeting for this purpose, then present and voting, upon men only who are eligible under Section 1 of this Statute, and who have been formally nominated for the honor by an active member, having first signified to the Keeper of the Signet, upon inquiry, his willingness to accept the membership.

Section 7.   Each person who shall be elected and received as a member of the Order in whatsoever manner, by virtue of any Statute now existing, or which may hereafter be established, shall by accepting membership be understood to engage to duly conform to all Statutes established from time to time for the government of the Order.

PENNSYLVANIA SOCIETY OF COLONIAL GOVERNORS
Incorporated July 6, 1910
Object

The purpose for which the corporation is formed is to promote interest in the history of the settlement and government of the American Colonies and the establishment of their Independence.

Membership

Adult male American citizens lineally descended from a Governor, Deputy or Lieutenant Governor, or one acting as a Governor, shall be eligible for membership.   Nominations for membership shall be made in writing by two members who shall send such proposal to the Secretary and he shall present the same to the Council who may authorize the Secretary to issue application form to the applicant and upon the same being duly executed and returned to the Secretary he shall deliver the same to the Committee on Membership and upon their approval and report of the same to the Council the latter may elect such applicant a member, a unanimous vote being required.   New members shall pay dues for the ensuing year.   Any member may be expelled by a two-thirds vote of the Council for any cause deemed derogatory to the interests of the Society.

REGULAR AND VOLUNTEER ARMY AND NAVY UNION

Information as to Objects and Requirements for Membership not available at time of publication.

SCIONS OF COLONIAL CAVALIERS

Objects

The purpose of the formation of the Society of Scions of Colonial Cavaliers is first to set the Colonial Cavalier right in American history, too much importance having been accredited to the Puritan by various of our national historians in treating of the founding and growth of our commonwealth. Secondly, our object pursuant to the thoughtful study of American history, is to compile records and erect memorials honoring the Colonial Cavaliers and if occasion offers, to render philanthropic aid to our country in times of war.

Membership

The membership of the society is divided into two parts. The first, the Palatines, the descendants of the Cavaliers who settled in America before 1650 and who were sons, grandsons or themselves members of the British nobility. The ordinary and sometimes vulgarly heralded "descent from kings" on the part of Americans, when the "king" dated back further than being at least the grandfather of one's pioneer Cavalier ancestor, counts for nothing, to bolster up one's claims for membership. The second order, The Landgraves, are members descended from distinguished Cavalier families of British gentry antecedents who settled in this country prior to the Revolution. Besides having a properly accredited invitation from the society, in addition to the above rigid requirements, the candidate for membership whether Palatine, or Landgrave, must also be a descendant of an ancestor of Cavalier antecedents who was a personage of note in the eighteenth century and also from one whose career complies with the same conditions in the nineteenth century. A great many Southern families have a "tradition" that their forefathers were "Cavaliers," an expression often loosely used to mean gentlemen and ladies. But only the historic fact of one's being a scion of a forefather who was a partisan of Charles I against Cromwell, or belonged to a

47

family ranked as Cavaliers by a reliable historian is of any avail for membership.

The issues between Charles I and his parliament are to us of today no longer living ones and had it not been for the fact that the Cavaliers and their progeny did a great deal toward building up our national polity, there would have been no adequate raison d'etre for the formation of our Society, however much the courtly manners of the Cavaliers and dignified mode of living on their estates might appeal to us. The American Revolution, with all the good it wrought in the cause of freedom, with Washington and others of eminent Colonial Cavalier lineage in the thickest of the fray, we do not enter into the discussion of pro or con, leaving that theme to other patriotic societies. Anyone who reads the signs of the times can discern that the dominant trend of thought at the present hour is Cavalier rather than Puritanical. The Puritan loved a village —and village gossip; the Cavalier, life on a landed estate where he was monarch of all he surveyed.

SOCIETY OF AMERICAN WARS OF THE UNITED STATES

Founded January 11, 1897

Objects

The Society of American Wars is organized for the purpose of paying just homage to the memory of those who conquered that we might live, and to inculcate and foster in all citizens that love of country and flag and that ambition for honorable achievement upon which so largely depends the maintenance of our high position among nations.

Membership

Section 1. An applicant for membership in the Society must be a man not less than twenty-one years of age, of good moral character and reputation, who is:

(a). A lineal descendant of an ancestor who served as a Governor, Lieutenant- or Deputy-Governor of any of the thirteen colonies.

(b). A lineal descendant of a member of the Councils or Assemblies or Councils of War of any of the thirteen colonies.

Pennsylvania Society of
Colonial Governors

Order of Indian Wars
of the United States

Society of Sons of the
Revolution

Navy League of the
United States

PLATE VIII

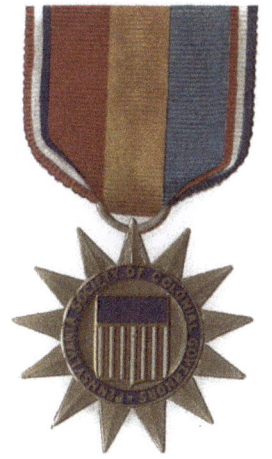

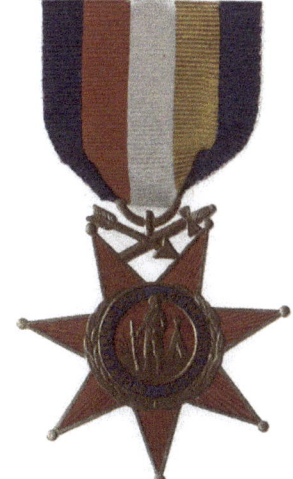

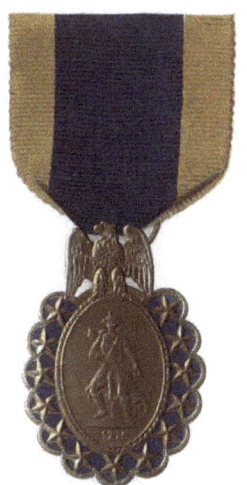

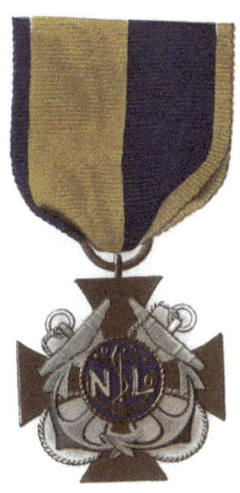

(c). A lineal descendant of a military or naval officer under authority of the colonies which afterwards formed the United States, from the settlement of Jamestown, May 13, 1607, to April 19, 1783.

(d). A military or naval officer who has served with honor as a commissioned officer of the United States in the Army, Navy, Marine Corps or Revenue Cutter Service, in any war in which the United States has been or shall be engaged or a lineal descendant thereof.

(e). A lineal descendant of a Companion of the Society of American Wars.

SOCIETY OF THE COLONIAL DAMES OF AMERICA

Organized April 8th, 1891

Objects

To collect manuscripts, traditions, relics and mementoes of bygone days for preservation, . . . commemorate the success of the American Revolution and consequent birth of our glorious Republic; diffuse healthful and intelligent information in whatever concerns the past and tends to create popular interest in American history and with a true spirit of patriotism seek to inspire genuine love of country in every heart within its range of influence, and to teach the young that it is a sacred obligation to do justice and honor to heroic ancestors whose ability, valor, sufferings and achievements are beyond all praise.

Members

Women who are descended in their own right from some ancestor of worthy life who came to reside in an American Colony prior to 1776, which ancestor or some one of his descendants, being a lineal descendant of the applicant, shall have rendered efficient service to his country during the Colonial period, either in the founding of a commonwealth, or of an institution which has survived and developed into importance, or who shall have held important position in the Colonial government, and who by distinguished services shall have contributed to the founding of this great and powerful nation. Services rendered after 1783 not recognized.

SOCIETY OF MAYFLOWER DESCENDANTS

Organized December 22d, 1894

Objects

Whereas, Our ancestors, passengers on "The Mayflower," landed in December, 1620, on Plymouth Rock, Massachusetts, and

Whereas, They came to settle in a new land and to found a new home and government, for the benefit of themselves and their posterity, and

Whereas, After struggles and hardships, which in the first year after their landing carried off one-half of their number and necessitated years of continued bravery and fortitude against innumerable trials of the severest kind, and

Whereas, Their acts and example have been instrumental in the establishment of Civil and Religious Liberty throughout this land,

Therefore, This Society is formed by lineal descendants of that band of Pilgrims, to preserve their memory, their records, their history, and all facts relating to them, their ancestors, and their posterity.

Membership

Every descendant over eighteen years of age of any Passenger on the "Mayflower," on the voyage which ended at Plymouth in December, 1620, is eligible to membership.

After the formation of a Society in any State, all persons residing in such State desiring to join the Society of Mayflower Descendants, shall do so through the local State Society.

Applicants for membership must be nominated and seconded by two members, and letters recommending the Applicant from both proposer and seconder must accompany the application, and must state that they are personally acquainted.

All preliminary applications must be approved by the Membership Committee, who investigate the social and moral standing of the Applicant. If the decision of the Committee is favorable they report the name of the Applicant to the Board of Assistants at a subsequent meeting, and upon such report pedigree blanks are issued upon which must be set out in detail each generation in descent from a Mayflower Passenger.

Every step in the pedigree must be proven by reference to published works recognized by the Society as authoritative, giving in each instance the volume and page quoted or by filing certified copies of Town or Church records, tombstone inscriptions or other unpublished evidence. No fact can be accepted which is based solely upon family or local traditions.

The pedigree blanks must be filled out in duplicate and sworn to before a Notary Public or other competent officer and sent to the Historian. After examination and approval by him and by the Historian General he will report to the Board of Assistants who will elect the Applicant a member of the Society unless in the meantime something prejudicial has been learned.

SOCIETY OF SONS OF THE REVOLUTION

Instituted February 22d, 1876,
Reorganized December 4th, 1883

Objects

It being evident, from a steady decline of a proper celebration of the National holidays of the United States of America, that popular concern in the events and men of the War of the Revolution is gradually declining, and that such lack of interest is attributable, not so much to the lapse of time and the rapidly increasing flood of immigration from foreign countries, as to the neglect, on the part of descendants of Revolutionary heroes, to perform their duty in keeping before the public mind the memory of the services of their ancestors and of the times in which they lived; therefore, the Society of the Sons of the Revolution has been instituted to perpetuate the memory of the men who, in the military, naval and civil service of the Colonies and of the Continental Congress by their acts or counsel, achieved the Independence of the country, and to further the proper celebration of the anniversaries of the birthday of Washington, and of prominent events connected with the War of the Revolution; to collect and secure for preservation the rolls, records, and other documents relating to that period; to inspire the members of the Society with the patriotic spirit of their forefathers; and to promote the feeling of friendship among them.

Membership

Any male person above the age of twenty-one years, of good character, and a descendant of one who, as a military, naval, or marine officer, soldier, sailor, or marine, in actual service, under the authority of any of the thirteen Colonies or States or of the Continental Congress, and remaining always loyal to such authority, or a descendant of one who signed the Declaration of Independence, or of one who, as a member of the Continental Congress or of the Congress of any of the Colonies or States, or as an official appointed by or under the authority of any such legislative bodies, actually assisted in the establishment of American Independence by services rendered during the War of the Revolution, becoming thereby liable to conviction of treason against the Government of Great Britain, but remainng always loyal to the authority of the Colonies or States, shall be eligible to membership in the Society.

SOCIETY OF THE ARMY OF SANTIAGO DE CUBA

Objects

To record the history and conserve the memory of the events of the campaign which resulted in the surrender on the 17th day of July, 1898, of the Spanish army, the City of Santiago de Cuba and the military province to which it pertained.

Membership

The membership of the Society shall consist of all officers and soldiers of the United States Army (including Acting Assistant Surgeons and authorized Volunteer Aides) who constituted the expeditionary force to Santiago de Cuba and who worthily participated in the campaign between the dates of June 14th and July 17th, 1898, and who shall signify their wish for membership by making application and paying the dues.

There shall be three classes of membership, namely: Original Members, Members by Inheritance, Members by Succession.

Military Order of the
Carabao

Medal of Honor of the
United States
of America

National Society
of the Children of the
American Revolution

Society of Mayflower
Descendants

The Order of Colonial
Lords of Manors
in America

PLATE IX

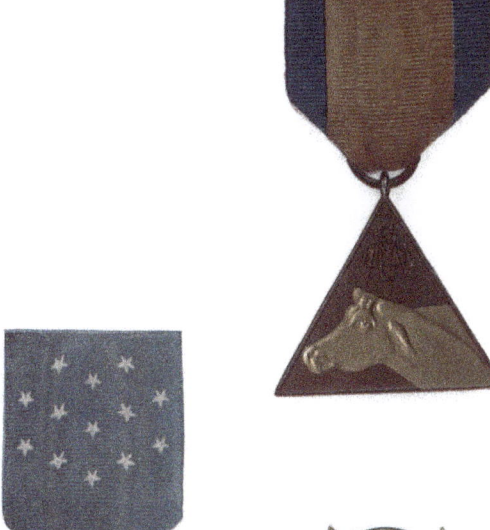

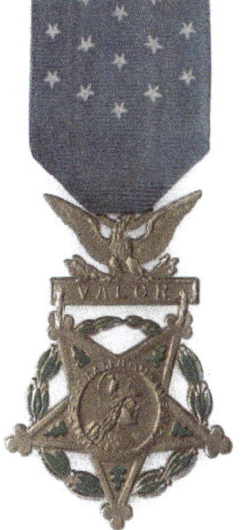

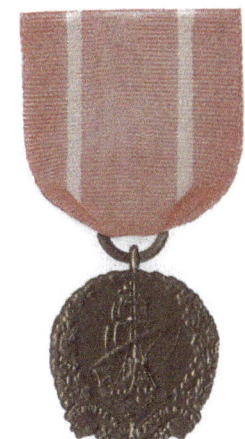

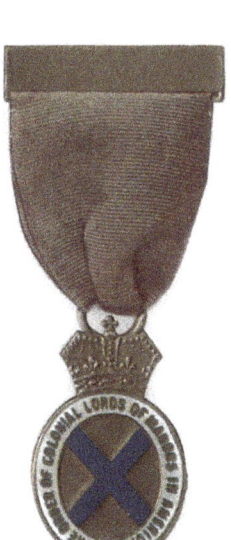

SOCIETY OF THE ARMY OF THE CUMBERLAND

Organized February 6th, 1868

Objects

To perpetuate the memory of the fortunes and achievements of the Army of the Cumberland; to preserve that unanimity of loyal sentiment and that kind and cordial feeling which has been an eminent characteristic of this army, and the main element of the power and success of its efforts in behalf of the cause of the Union. The history and glory of the officers and soldiers belonging to this army, who have fallen either on the field of battle or otherwise in the line of their duty, shall be a permanent trust to this Society, and every effort shall be made to collect and preserve the proper memorials of their services, to inscribe their names upon the roll of honor, and to transmit their fame to posterity. It shall also be the object and bounden duty of this Society to relieve, as far as possible, the families of such deceased officers and soldiers, when in indigent circumstances, either by the voluntary contribution of the members, or in such other manner as they may determine, when the cases are brought to their attention. This provision shall also hereafter apply to the suffering families of those members of the Society who may in the future be called hence, and the welfare of the soldier's widow and orphan shall forever be a holy trust in the hands of his surviving comrades.

Membership

Composed of officers and soldiers who served with honor in the Army of the Cumberland.

SOCIETY OF THE ARMY OF THE OHIO

Instituted December 15th, 1868

Objects

To preserve and perpetuate the history of the Army of the Ohio; to preserve and unite those patriotic sentiments, and to maintain and strengthen that courteous and friendly intercourse for which the members of this army have always been distinguished. To preserve the name and fame of the members of this army who have fallen in the field, or otherwise perished in the service of their country, shall be one of the sacred duties of this Association, and no efforts shall be spared to collect and preserve, in the archives of the Society, the testimonials of their deeds and services.

This Society tenders to the widows and orphans of our fallen comrades its warmest sympathy, and sacredly pledges itself to provide for the wants and relieve the sufferings of all such as are destitute, by the voluntary contributions of the members, or in such other way as may from time to time be determined. It further pledges itself to use all proper effort, and procure for all such disabled soldiers, and their families, as are entitled thereto, the pensions now provided by law. The welfare of the soldier's widow, the good name and education of his children, shall always be regarded as a sacred trust of the Association.

Membership

All such officers and soldiers as have at any time served in this army, and who have been honorably discharged from such service; or who remain in service in the regular army, who shall have subscribed to the Constitution and By-Laws of the Society, and paid their initiation fee.

Honorary members may, from time to time, be elected from among the officers of other armies of the United States who have served with distinction in their armies.

SOCIETY OF THE CINCINNATI
Instituted May 10th, 1783

The historic and patriotic Order of the Cincinnati was founded by the American and French officers at the cantonments of the Continental Army on the Hudson at the close of hostilities in the War of the Revolution for American Independence, May 10, 1783.

In forming the society it was declared that, "To perpetuate, therefore, as well the remembrance of this vast event, as the mutual friendships which have been formed under the pressure of common danger, and, in many instances, cemented by the blood of the parties, the officers of the American Army do, hereby, in the most solemn manner, associate, constitute, and combine themselves into one Society of Friends, to endure as long as they shall endure, or any of their eldest male posterity, and, in failure thereof, the collateral branches who may be judged worthy of becoming its supporters and members."

For convenience, thirteen State societies were formed, and one in France, under the direct patronage of Louis XVI, which was dispersed at the Reign of Terror in 1793. Upon the roll of original members appeared the names of all the great historic military and naval characters of the Revolution, and upon the roll of honorary members, elected for their own lives only, appeared many of the signers of the Declaration of Independence.

Membership

All Continental officers who had served with honor and resigned after three years' service as officers, or who had been rendered supernumerary and honorably discharged, in one of the several reductions of the American Army, or who had continued to the end of the war, and all French officers who had served in the co-operating army under Count d'Estaing, or auxiliary army under Count de Rochambeau, and held or attained the rank of colonel for such services, or who had commanded a French fleet or ship of war on the American coast, were entitled to become original members, and upon doing so were required to contribute a month's pay.

State Societies

The Cincinnati is organically one society in membership, but for convenience in admission of members and in its charitable and patriotic objects was subdivided into State societies by the Institution of 1783, there being thirteen. Six dissolved societies were restored to membership by the General Society in triennial meeting since 1902.

Membership descends to the eldest lineal male descendant, if judged worthy, and, in failure of direct male descent, to male descendants through intervening female descendants. The Institution gives the same right to the proper descendant of any Continental officer who was killed or died in service.

The general society when legislating for the good of the Order is composed of the general officers and five delegates from every State society, and meets triennially. In 1854 it ruled that proper descendants of Revolutionary officers who were entitled to original membership, but who never could avail themselves of it, are qualified for hereditary membership, if found worthy, on due application.

SOCIETY OF THE DAUGHTERS OF HOLLAND DAMES

Founded May, 1895

Objects

The objects of the Society shall be to perpetuate the memory and to promote the principles of the Dutch ancestors of its members, to collect documents, genealogical and historical, relating to the Dutch in America, and to erect commemorative and durable memorials to be lasting tributes to the early Dutch settlers.

Membership

Any woman shall be eligible for membership who is above the age of eighteen years, lineally descended from a Hollander (Nederlander), resident of New Netherland previous to the Treaty of Westminster, 1674, and who has been adjudged worthy and acceptable to the Society.

The admitting ancestor must have been a man born in the Netherlands, of Holland parentage and must have been either:

(a) A Director General of New Netherland;

(b) A member of Council of the Director General of New Netherland;

(c) A member of a Representative Body, Religious or Secular, of New Netherland;

(d) A Patroon or a Freeholder of New Netherland;

(e) A Commissioner in New Netherland, either of Indian affairs, of Boundaries or of Treaties;

(f) A Commissioned officer, soldier or sailor who served in defence of the Colonies.

The fact, not the date of his services, shall establish the claim.

The family of the ancestor must have come from some place included in the Netherlands, according to their boundaries in 1555.*

*Authority: Blok's History of the People of the Netherlands, especially Map of 1550.

56

SOCIETY OF THE PORTO RICAN EXPEDITION

Information as to Objects and Requirements for Membership not available at time of publication.

SOCIETY OF THE UNITED STATES DAUGHTERS—
1776-1812

Objects

Whereas, In all time and in all ages, valor, patriotism and self-sacrifice have been justly held as the triune virtues which constitute true heroism; and

Whereas, Next to the approval of God and our conscience, the approval of our fellowmen must ever remain the incentive to great and noble deeds; therefore be it

Resolved, That in recalling the deeds of those who in 1776 sacrificed fortune and life itself in the defense of their liberties, and of those who, in 1812, in the face of like hardships and discouragements, settled forever the question of our national Independence, the United States Daughters of 1776 and 1812 honor themselves, and hold up to their children examples of disinterested patriotism, steadfastness in adversity, and unflinching courage in defense of right, which will, we trust, influence their lives in whatever paths an all-wise Providence may lead them.

It is therefore, the aim and purpose of this Society to collect such papers, letters and documents as shall help to write a true and impartial history of our country; to honor the graves of those patriots who gave their lives to the good cause; to promote friendly and social relations between the descendants of those who made that history possible, and for such other worthy objects as the Society, from time to time, may judge wise and proper.

Membership

Any white woman shall be eligible to membership in the United States Daughters of 1776-1812, who is lineally descended from an ancestor who, either as a military, naval or marine officer, soldier, sailor or marine, or an official, or in any effective way and with unfailing loyalty, assisted in establishing American Independence during the wars of 1776 and 1812; provided she be of good moral character, and shall be judged worthy of becoming a member.

SONS OF VETERANS, UNITED STATES OF AMERICA

Objects

Founded upon a trust in Almighty God, with a realization that under His beneficent guidance the free institutions of our land, consecrated by the services and blood of our fathers, have been preserved, and upon a true allegiance to the government of the United States of America, pledging fidelity to law and order, this Association declares its objects to be:

First. To perpetuate the memory of the sacrifices of our fathers and forefathers and their services for the maintenance of the Union.

Second. To inculcate patriotism, to teach truthful history, and to spread and sustain the doctrine of equal rights, universal liberty and justice to all.

Third. To assist the members of the Grand Army of the Republic, and all honorably discharged Union Soldiers, Sailors and Marines of the War of the Rebellion of 1861-1865; to extend aid and protection to their widows and orphans, and to honor the memories of the heroic dead through historical exercises and the proper observance of Memorial and Union Defenders' Days.

Fourth. To aid and assist worthy and needy members of our Order.

Membership

All male descendants, whether through the paternal or maternal line, not less than eighteen years of age, of Soldiers, Sailors or Marines, who were regularly mustered and served honorably in, or who were honorably discharged from, the Army or Navy of the United States of America, during the War of the Rebellion of 1861-65; and who have never been convicted of any infamous or heinous crime, or who have, or whose ancestors through whom membership is claimed, have never voluntarily borne arms against the Government of the United States of America.

SWEDISH COLONIAL SOCIETY

Organized February 5th, 1909

Objects

The object of the Society shall be to collect, preserve, and publish records, documents, and other material, printed or in manuscript, and to commemorate events relating to the history of Swedes in America.

Membership

Any male person over twenty-one years of age, of good character, shall be eligible to membership. All members shall be elected by the Council, who shall have power to suspend or expel any member who in their judgment may have conducted himself in an improper manner.

THE AMERICAN CROSS OF HONOR

Organized 1898.   Incorporated by Act of Congress 1906

Object

To advocate those great principles of the value and sanctity of human life and the best means of preserving it.

Membership

The regular membership is composed of persons upon whom the United States Government has conferred the life-saving medal of honor.

Bronze crosses of honor are conferred in certain cases where great heroism is shown in saving human life. A gold cross of honor is awarded in exceptional cases to persons who by great daring have highly distinguished themselves in saving life. This cross also is conferred biennially upon some person nominated by the Royal National Life-Boat Institution of Great Britain for the most heroic service in saving life; the person thus honored must have received the gold life-saving medal of the said institution.

The President of the United States is Honorary President of the order. M. Armand Faillières, ex-President of France; the German Emperor, the King of Great Britain, the King of Italy, ex-Presidents Roosevelt and Taft, and Andrew Carnegie are honorary members.

THE AMERICAN NATIONAL RED CROSS

Objects

To furnish volunteer aid to the sick and wounded of armies in time of war, in accordance with the spirit and conditions of the conference of Geneva, of October, 1863, and also of the treaty of the Red Cross, or the treaty of Geneva, of August 22d, 1864, to which the United States of America gave its adhesion on March 1st, 1882.

And for said purposes to perform all the duties devolved upon a national society by each nation which has acceded to said treaty.

To act in matters of voluntary relief and in accord with the military and naval authorities as a medium of communication between the people of the United States of America and their Army and Navy, and to act in such matters between similar national societies of other governments through the "Comité International de Secours," and the Government and the people and the Army and Navy of the United States of America.

And to continue and carry on a system of national and international relief in time of peace and to apply the same in mitigating the sufferings caused by pestilence, famine, fire, floods and other great national calamities, and to devise and carry on measures for preventing the same.

Membership

Individual membership in the American National Red Cross consists of the following classes:

(a) Annual Members. Any citizen or resident of the United States or its dependencies may become a member of the American National Red Cross upon application to the Central Committee or a Chapter and the payment of one dollar to the National Treasurer, or to the Treasurer of the Chapter in whose jurisdiction the applicant resides, and may continue such membership by the annual payment of the same amount. Provided, That the Central Committee, as respects any member at large, or the Executive Committee of any Chapter, as respects any chapter membership, shall have authority, for reasons satisfactory to itself, to terminate membership at any time by notice. Annual members who do not live within the jurisdiction of any Chapter or who do not connect themselves with a Chapter, shall

Colonial Daughters of
the XVII Century

The General Society
of Colonial Wars

Association of Military
Surgeons
of the United States

United Sons of
Confederate Veterans

The
Saint Nicholas Society
of the City of New York

PLATE X

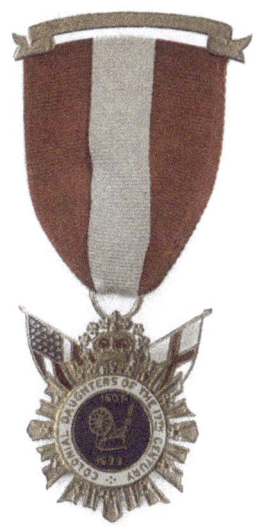

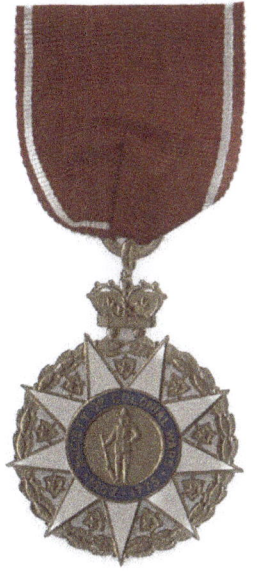

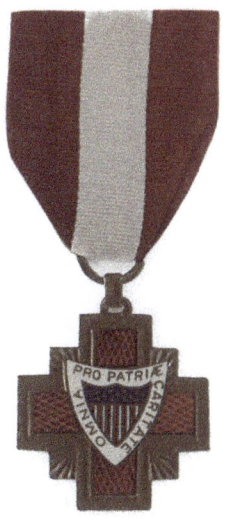

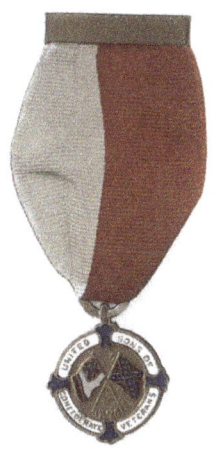

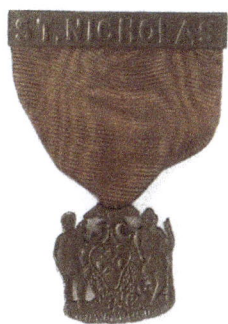

be members at large and shall pay their annual dues directly to the national office in Washington. Unless he otherwise requests, any member of the Red Cross residing within the jurisdiction of a Chapter shall be presumed to affiliate with the Chapter and shall be expected to pay his annual dues to the Chapter.

(b) Subscribing Members. Any citizen or resident of the United States or of its dependencies may become a subscribing member of the American National Red Cross on application to the Central Committee or a Chapter and the payment of two dollars per annum.

(c) Contributing Members. Any citizen or resident of the United States or of its dependencies may become a contributing member of the American National Red Cross on application to the Central Committee or a Chapter and the payment of five dollars per annum.

(d) Sustaining Members. Any citizen or resident of the United States or of its dependencies may become a sustaining member of the American National Red Cross on application to the Central Committee or a Chapter and the payment of ten dollars per annum.

(e) Life Members. Any citizen or resident of the United States or of its dependencies may become a life member of the American National Red Cross on application to the Central Committee or a Chapter and the payment of twenty-five dollars.

(f) Patrons. Any citizen or resident of the United States or of its dependencies may become a Patron of the American National Red Cross upon application to the Central Committee or a Chapter and the payment of one hundred dollars.

(g) Any nurse enrolled in the Red Cross Nursing Service shall by such enrollment become a member of the American National Red Cross without payment of dues.

(h) Honorary Members. Those who have rendered specially meritorious or distinguished service to the association and have been approved for such distinction by two-thirds vote of the members present at any annual meeting of the General Board, shall become honorary members.

THE COLONIAL SOCIETY OF MASSACHUSETTS

Incorporated December 29th, 1892

Objects

For the purpose of collecting and preserving mementoes of our Colonial Ancestors; propagating knowledge of their lives and deeds by the publication of ancient documents and records; cultivating an interest in the history of our Country, and more especially of the Colonies of Plymouth and The Massachusetts Bay; encouraging individual research into the part taken by our forefathers in the building of our Nation; promoting intelligent discussion of events in which the people of our Commonwealth have been concerned, in order that justice may be done to participants and false claims silenced; and inspiring among our members a spirit of fellowship based upon a proper appreciation of our common ancestry.

Membership

The number of Resident Members of the Society never shall exceed one hundred. They shall be elected from among the citizens of Massachusetts, and shall cease to be members whenever they cease to be residents thereof. The number of Corresponding Members never shall exceed fifty; and the number of Honorary Members never shall exceed twenty. They shall be elected from among non-residents of Massachusetts, and shall cease to be members if at any time they become both citizens and permanent residents thereof. No person shall be eligible to membership who cannot prove, by documentary evidence satisfactory to the Council, his lineal descent from an ancestor who was a resident of the Colonies of Plymouth or The Massachusetts Bay.

THE GENERAL SOCIETY OF COLONIAL WARS

Objects

Whereas, It is desirable that there should be adequate celebrations commemorative of the events of Colonial history, happening from the settlement of Jamestown, Va., May 13, 1607, to the battle of Lexington, April 19, 1775;

Therefore, The Society of Colonial Wars has been instituted to perpetuate the memory of those events, and of the men who, in military, naval and civil positions of high trust and responsibilty, by their acts or counsel, assisted in the establishment, defense and preservation of the American Colonies, and were in truth founders of this Nation. With this end in view, it seeks to collect and preserve manuscripts, rolls, relics and records; to provide suitable commemorations or memorials relating to the American Colonial period, and to inspire in its members the fraternal and patriotic spirit of their forefathers, and in the community respect and reverence for those whose public services made our freedom and unity possible.

Membership

Any male person above the age of twenty-one years, of good moral character and reputation, shall be eligible to membership in the Society of Colonial Wars, who is lineally descended, in the male or female line, from an ancestor:

(1) Who served as a military or naval officer, or as a soldier, sailor or marine, or as a privateersman, under authority of the Colonies which afterward formed the United States, or in the forces of Great Britain which participated with those of the said Colonies in any wars in which the said colonies were engaged, or in which they enrolled men, from the settlement of Jamestown, May 13, 1607, to the battle of Lexington, April 19, 1775; or,

(2) Who held office in any of the Colonies between the dates above mentioned, either as

(a) Director-General, Vice-Director-General, or member of the Council or legislative body in the Colony of New Netherlands.

(b) Governor, Lieutenant- or Deputy-Governor, Lord Proprietor, member of the King's or Governor's Council, or legislative body in the Colonies of New York, New Jersey, Virginia, Pennsylvania and Delaware.

(c) Lord Proprietor, Governor, Deputy-Governor, or member of the Council or of the legislative body in Maryland and the Carolinas.

(d) Governor, Deputy-Governor, Governor's Assistant, or Commissioner to the United Colonies of New England, or member of the Council, body of Assistants, or legislative body in any of the New England Colonies.

One collateral representative of an ancestor, such as above specified, shall be eligible for membership, provided there be no existing lineal descendant, and provided that such person be the oldest collateral representative in the male line of such ancestor, or has filed with the Secretary-General of the Society written renunciation from all other persons having nearer claims to representation.

No State Society shall adopt any rule of eligibility for membership which shall admit any person not eligible for membership in the General Society; but any State Society may, except as to members transferred from another State Society, further restrict at its discretion the basis of eligibility for membership in its own Society.

THE HEREDITARY ORDER OF DESCENDANTS OF COLONIAL GOVERNORS PRIOR TO 1750

Chartered
(Founded 1896)

Purposes

To commemorate the services of those men who singly exercised supreme executive power in the American Colonies and who laid in them the foundations of stable government and of that respect for civil law and authority which made the maintenance of their future independence possible.

Objects

I.   To further, in so far as convenable, all wise, just, free and humane patriotic objects, and objects of patriotic societies.

II.   Historical, genealogical, literary and social, and especially the awakening and increase of general interest in the history, customs and traditions of the Colonial Period.

Membership

Membership is purely honorary and is by invitation only. Both men and women are included.

Colonial Society of
Pennsylvania

Military Order of the
Midnight Sun

Grand Army of the
Republic

Society of the Army
of the Cumberland

The Order
of Washington

PLATE XI

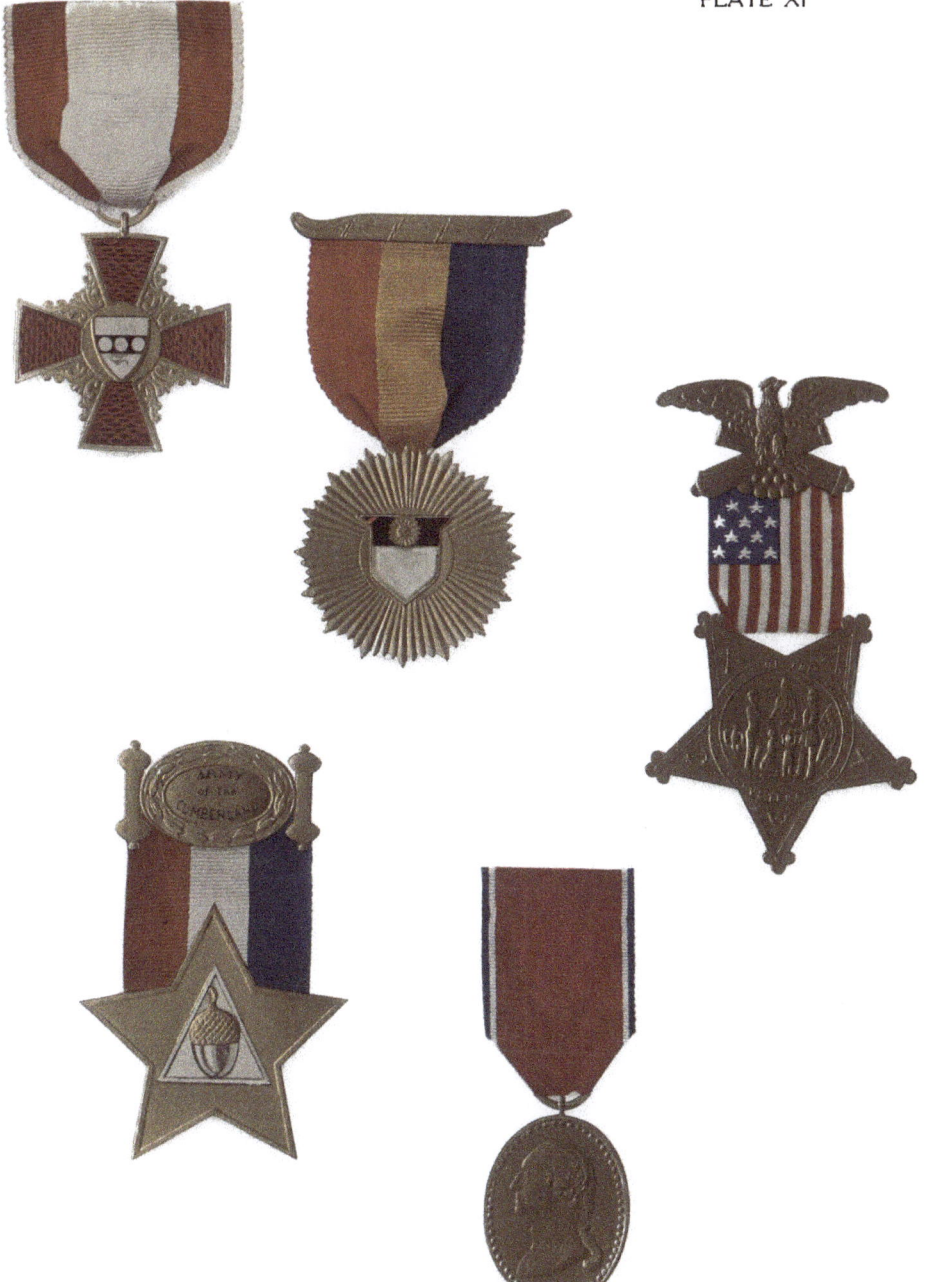

THE HOLLAND SOCIETY OF NEW YORK

Organized March 21, 1885
Incorporated May 12th, 1885

Objects

First.   To collect and preserve information respecting the early history and settlement of the City and State of New York by the Dutch, and to discover, collect and preserve all still existing documents, etc., relating to their genealogy and history.

Second.   To perpetuate the memory and foster and promote the principles and virtues of the Dutch ancestors of its members, and to promote social intercourse among the latter.

Third.   To gather by degrees a library for the use of the Society, composed of all obtainable books, monographs, pamphlets, manuscripts, etc., relating to the Dutch in America.

Fourth.   To cause statedly to be prepared and read before the Society, papers, essays, etc., on questions in the history or genealogy of the Dutch in America.

Fifth.   To cause to be prepared and published when the requisite materials have been discovered and procured, collections for a memorial history of the Dutch in America, wherein shall be particularly set forth the part belonging to that element in the growth and development of American character, institutions and progress.

Membership

Section 1.   No one shall be eligible as a member unless he be of full age, of respectable standing in society, of good moral character, and the descendant in the direct male line of a Dutchman who was a native or resident of New York or of the American colonies prior to the year 1675. This shall include those of other former nationalities who found in Holland a refuge or a home, and whose descendants in the male line came to this country as Dutch settlers, speaking Dutch as their native tongue. This shall also include descendants in the male line of Dutch settlers who were born within the limits of Dutch settlements, and the descendants in the male line of persons who possessed the right of Dutch citizenship within Dutch settlements in America, prior to the year 1675; also of any descendant in the direct male line of a Dutchman, one of whose descendants became a member of this Society prior to June 16, 1886.

So long as there are one thousand members of the Society no further elections to membership shall be held, but candidates for admission shall be placed in order upon a waiting list; provided, however, that this restriction shall not prevent the immediate election of any candidate who is the descendant of a present or former member of the Society.

Badge adopted March 30, 1887

The most significant medal, from an historical point of view, which was ever struck in Holland, is the so-called "Beggars' Medal." It is the memorial of the very first steps of that march toward civil and religious liberty in which the men of the Netherlands, after heroic struggles, finally led the world. And, therefore, it is a most appropriate token for us to wear, who have received in largest measure, in this New Republic, the benefits of the noble conflict of our Dutch forefathers.

"The gourd or bottle had its origin from the usage made of it by the pilgrims—that class of people who, to perform a penance or to fulfill certain vows, undertake a journey to the distant shrine of some saint, like that of St. James in Spain or of Loretto in Italy. They are obliged to go there begging by the way, and they carry this bottle-gourd, or calabash, attached to the girdle, for the purpose of carrying water for their use when they have to traverse dry and arid parts of the country. For this reason these allied nobles made use both of the porringer and the wallet as an emblem of poverty, and to turn into pleasantry the name of beggars, which had been given to them with so much indignity. This is not all. These lords, wishing to engrave on each other's memory the vow which each had made to defend the privileges of the country, even to carry the wallet, took pride in wearing on the breast certain medals attached to ribbons, and very often joined with a porringer and a gourd."

The form adopted by The Holland Society is a facsimile of the one to which are attached two such porringers and a gourd or bottle, and shows on its face the armed bust of Philip II. of Spain, with the first half of the motto, "En Tout Fidelles Au Roy," and on the reverse two wallets, between the straps of which are two hands joined, with the remainder of the motto, "Jusques a Porter La Besace," together with the date, 1566, the figures of which are, however, separated, one in each corner formed by the crossed hands and wallets.

66

"THE HUGUENOT SOCIETY OF AMERICA"

Founded April 12, 1883. Incorporated June 12, 1885

Objects

First, To perpetuate the memory and to foster and promote the principles and virtues of the Huguenots.

Secondly, To publicly commemorate the principal events in the history of the Huguenots.

Thirdly, To discover, collect and preserve all existing documents, monuments, etc., relating to the genealogy or history of the Huguenots of America.

Fourthly, To gather by degrees a library, for the use of the Society, composed of all obtainable books, monographs, pamphlets, manuscripts, etc., relating to the Huguenots.

Fifthly, To cause to be prepared and read before the Society, papers, essays, etc., on questions in the history or genealogy of the Huguenots; their settlements, biographies, public acts, influence on the society, arts, commerce and politics of America especially, and of other countries where they settled.

Sixthly, To cause to be prepared and published a series of volumes entitled "Collections of the Huguenot Society of America."

Seventhly, To establish branches of this Society in other American cities and to encourage the foundation of similar Societies in other countries where the Huguenots have taken refuge.

Membership

Section 1. The following classes of persons are eligible for nomination to membership in the Society:

First, Descendants in the male or female line of the Huguenot families who emigrated to America prior to the Promulgation of the Edict of Toleration, November 28th, 1787, or who left France for other countries than America prior to that date, may be elected as regular members.

Secondly, Persons who have made the history, genealogy, principles, etc., of the Huguenots a special subject of study and research, and have written and published the same, may be elected as regular members.

Thirdly, Persons who have rendered some conspicuous service in the advancement of Huguenot interests may be elected as honorary members. They shall have no vote.

Fourthly, Persons who are residents of foreign countries may be elected as corresponding members. They shall have no vote.

Section 2. Regular members shall be either life members upon the payment of the initiation fee of $10 on joining the Society, and $50 in that or in any one year thereafter, or annual members upon the payment of the initiation fee of $10 besides the annual dues of $5 for the first year and $5 annually thereafter. The annual dues shall be payable in advance on the 13th day of April of each year. Notice shall be sent by the Treasurer to every member failing to pay his annual subscription when due. If such annual dues shall be in arrears for two years and shall not be paid in full, after due notice as aforesaid, on or before the first day of June following the day upon which the second year's dues become payable, the person so failing to pay shall cease to be a member of the Society and his or her name shall be erased from the list of members accordingly, provided, however, that the Executive Committee shall have power in their discretion to restore such delinquent member upon payment of the amount due and upon proof satisfactory to the Executive Committee that the failure to pay was due to oversight or excusable neglect.

Section 3. Part 1. Honorary and corresponding members shall be elected by the Society on recommendation of the Executive Committee, to whom all applications for such nominations should be addressed.

Part 2. Only members of the Society have the right of proposing and seconding candidates, and those members must have personally known such candidates for over a year, and vouch for their good standing. Application blanks for regular members will be furnished by the chairman of the Pedigree Committee. When these are filled in with the names of the candidate for admission, names of the Huguenot ancestor, and names of the proposer and seconder, and returned to the Library, the chairman, if satisfied that the Huguenot claims are admissable, shall then forward pedigree blanks.

Part 3. These pedigree blanks must be filled out in the most exact manner possible, and all dates of births, marriages and deaths given, before the name of the candidate can be con-

Society of
American Wars of the
United States

Order of Americans of
Armorial Ancestry

The Society of the
Army of West Virginia

The Society of the
Army of the James

The Society of the
Army of the Tennessee

PLATE XII

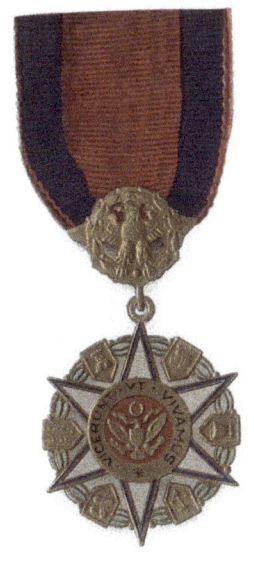

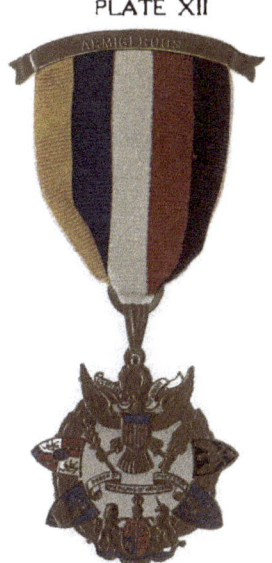

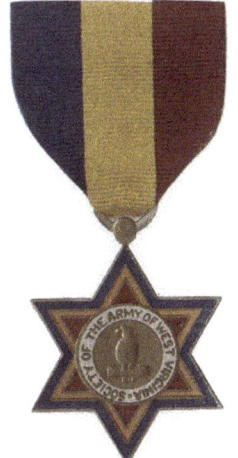

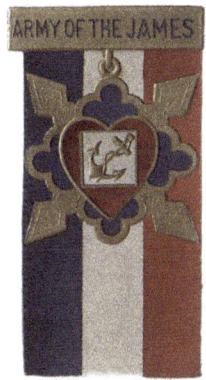

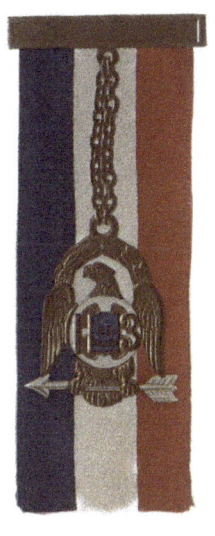

sidered by the Executive Committee. If printed records of these dates exist, page and book in which they appear must be given. If conclusive evidence be furnished that these records have been lost or destroyed, the committee may accept other satisfactory evidence.

Part 4. Candidates for regular membership must be proposed at a meeting of the Executive Committee. These candidates shall be elected by the Executive Committee at any meeting subsequent to that at which they were proposed on the affirmative vote of two-thirds of the committee present.

Part 5. All supplementary pedigrees must be approved by the Executive Committee before they can be filed in the archives of the Society, or before the names of the Huguenot ancestors mentioned therein can be inserted in the list of members.

Part 6. The Secretary shall (through the Treasurer) notify the candidate of his or her election and with this notification the Treasurer shall enclose the bill for initiation fee, and dues for the first year,—and upon the payment within thirty days of the required amount, the person shall be entered on the list of members. Due notification of the election of the candidate shall be sent to the proposer by the Secretary.

THE MILITARY ORDER OF THE LOYAL LEGION OF THE UNITED STATES

Instituted April 15, 1865

Objects

The objects of this Order shall be to cherish the memories and associations of the war waged in defence of the unity and indivisibility of the Republic; strengthen the ties of fraternal fellowship and sympathy formed by companionship-in-arms; advance the best interests of the soldiers and sailors of the United States especially of those associated as Companions of this Order, and extend all possible relief to their widows and children; foster the cultivation of military and naval science; enforce unqualified allegiance to the General Government; protect the rights and liberties of American citizenship, and maintain National Honor, Union and Independence.

Membership

Section 1.   The Companions of this Order shall be elected in the manner hereinafter provided from the classes defined in this Article, and shall be entitled Companions of the First Class, Second Class and Third Class, respectively, as described and defined.

Section 2.   Original Companions of the First Class. Commissioned officers and honorably discharged commissioned officers of the United States Army, Navy and Marine Corps, Regular or Volunteer, including officers of assimilated or corresponding rank by appointment of the Secretary of War or Navy, who were actually engaged in the suppression of the Rebellion prior to the fifteenth day of April, 1865, and whose names appear in the Official Registers of the United States Army and Navy and of the Volunteer Force of the United States Army, or appeared upon the official records of the United States War or Navy Department during their term of service as commissioned officers of organizations mustered into the service of the United States, and not restricted to service within any given State, for a period of service not less than ninety days, or who served under the President's call of the fifteenth day of April, 1861; or who, having served as non-commissioned officers, warrant officers or enlisted men, during the War of the Rebellion, have since been or may hereafter be commissioned as officers in the United States Regular or Volunteer Army, Navy or Marine Corps; and persons who, having served as non-commissioned officers, warrant officers or enlisted men as aforesaid, shall have become eligible to membership by descent from members of the Order, or officers who were eligible as such, who shall have died.   All midshipmen in the United States Navy and all cadets of the United States Army, who while pursuing their course in the United States Naval Academy or the United State Military Academy at West Point, actually rendered service, and which service has been or shall be recognized by the United States Congress or the Navy Department or by the War Department as service rendered during the War of the Rebellion.   Those elected under the provisions of this section shall be designated Original Companions of the First Class.

Section 3.   Hereditary Companions of the First Class. The direct male lineal descendants, who shall have attained the age of twenty-one years, of deceased Original Companions of the First Class, and of deceased officers not members of the

70

Order, but who were eligible as such, and whose direct descent shall in every case be traced anew from the original founder of the membership in the Order, or from the deceased eligible officer, and not otherwise. Those elected under the provisions of this section shall be designated Hereditary Companions of the First Class.

Section 4. Any Original Companion having no direct lineal male descendant, may, by writing, filed with the Recorder of his Commandery, nominate a Companion of the Second Class from among the collateral male members of his family, descending only from his own brother or sister, and the person so nominated when he shall have attained the age of twenty-one years shall become eligible to membership for life in the Second Class. Any nomination for membership in any class heretofore filed by an Original Companion shall be valid and effectual as a nomination under this Section.

Section 5. No eligibility to membership shall be derived from an Original Companion who has been expelled from the Order and not reinstated.

Section 6. The resignation of a Companion, or the dropping of a Companion from the rolls for neglect or refusal to pay arrears, or the expulsion of a Companion who has obtained membership by descent, shall not affect the eligibility of his successor.

Section 7. An applicant applying for membership by virtue of descent from a deceased Companion, or from a deceased eligible officer, shall file affidavits and furnish such other evidence as may be required, setting forth the facts upon which the eligibility is claimed.

Section 8. Second Class: The sons, and if there be no sons, the grandsons, of living Companions of the First Class, whether Original, in Succession, or by Inheritance, who shall have attained the age of twenty-one years, shall be eligible to membership. Those elected under the provisions of this Section shall be designated Companions of the Second Class.

Section 9. Upon the death of the Companion from whom his eligibility by direct descent was derived, a Companion of the Second Class shall become a Succession Companion of the First Class, and be so announced to the Order by Circular.

Section 10. Companions of the Second Class shall have the right to vote in all cases except in elections of applicants for membership as Original Companions of the First Class.

Section 11. Third Class: Companions of the Third Class are those gentlemen who, in civil life, during the Rebellion, were specially distinguished for conspicuous and consistent loyalty to the National Government, and were active and eminent in maintaining the supremacy of the same; and who, prior to the fifteenth day of April, 1890, were elected members of the Order pursuant to the then existing provisions of the Constitution, the power to elect such having ceased at that date.

THE NATIONAL MARY WASHINGTON MEMORIAL ASSOCIATION

Organized February 22d, 1890, for 1000 years

Objects

The particular objects of the Society are the erection of a suitable monument to Mary, the mother of George Washington, including the acquisition of such ground as may be proper, and the improvement thereof by enclosure and otherwise, and the maintenance and preservation in good order, in perpetuity, of said monument with the improvements.

Contributors

Any person who shall pay to the Treasurer annually the sum of one dollar or more shall be recorded as a contributor for that year and shall be published as such in the annual report of the Board of Directors.

Providing for a List of Life Members

35.—The payment of twenty-five dollars by one person at the same time shall entitle the person so paying to an Hereditary Life Membership in the Association, the certificate of which is a medal in the form of a star with the head of Mary, the mother of Washington, in the center, the initials of the Association (N. M. W. M. A.) in blue and white enamel upon the five points on the obverse side, and the Washington Heraldic colors on the reverse side.

This Association being organized for perpetuity, these Life Members, and their successors by inheritance, are privileged to aid in caring for the protection and preservation of the grave and monument of the mother of Washington for all future time. These medals are as an inheritance to descend from mother to daughter or granddaughter, and so on in the direct female line, or failing these, by will or deed, and entitle the inheritor to a vote at all meetings of the Association after February 22d, 1896.

No medals will be given out after that date.

THE NATIONAL SOCIETY OF THE COLONIAL DAMES OF AMERICA

Preamble

Whereas, History shows that the remembrance of a nation's glory in the past stimulates to national greatness in the future, and that successive generations are awakened to truer patriotism and aroused to noble endeavor by the contemplation of the heroic deeds of their forefathers; therefore, the Society of Colonial Dames of America has been formed, that the descendants of those men who in the Colonial period by their rectitude, courage, and self-denial prepared the way for success in that struggle which gained for the country its liberty and constitution, may associate themselves together to do honor to the virtues of their forefathers, and to encourage in all who come under their influence, true patriotism, built on a knowledge of the self-sacrifice and heroism of those men of the colonies who laid the foundation of this great nation.

Title

1. Name and Organization. This Society shall be known by the name, style and title of the National Society of the Colonial Dames of America, and shall be composed of Corporate Societies of which there are, the Societies in the Thirteen Colonial States, or the Ancestral Societies; the Society in the District of Columbia, or the Domicile or Charter Society; and the Societies in the Non-Colonial States, or the Associate Societies.

Every member of every State Society shall be a Dame of one of the Thirteen Ancestral Societies.

Objects

1. The objects of this Society shall be to collect and preserve manuscripts, traditions, relics, and mementos of bygone days; to preserve and restore buildings connected with the early history of our country, to diffuse healthful and intelligent information concerning the past, to create a popular interest in our Colonial history, to stimulate a spirit of true patriotism and a genuine love of country, and to impress upon the young the sacred obligation of honoring the memory of those heroic ancestors whose ability, valor, sufferings and achievements are beyond all praise.

Membership

1. Membership. The Corporate Societies shall be composed entirely of women who are descended in their own right from some ancestor of worthy life who came to reside in an American colony prior to 1750, which ancestor or some one of his descendants, being a lineal ascendant of the applicant, shall have rendered efficient service to his country during the Colonial period, either in the founding of a commonwealth, or of an institution which has survived and developed into importance, or who shall have held an important position in a Colonial government, or who, by distinguished services, shall have contributed to the founding of this great and powerful nation.

2. Date of Ancestor's Services. All services which constitute a claim to membership must have been rendered before July 5, 1776, but this date shall be held to include all the signers of the Declaration of Independence.

THE NATIONAL SOCIETY OF THE DAUGHTERS
OF THE AMERICAN REVOLUTION

Objects

1. To perpetuate the memory of the spirit of the men and women who achieved American Independence, by the acquisition and protection of historical spots, and the erection of monuments; by the encouragement of historical research in relation to the Revolution and the publication of its results; by the preservation of documents and relics, and of the records of the individual services of Revolutionary soldiers and patriots, and by the promotion of celebrations of all patriotic anniversaries.

2. To carry out the injunction of Washington in his farewell address to the American people, "to promote, as an object of primary importance, institutions for the general diffusion of knowledge," thus developing an enlightened public opinion, and affording to young and old such advantages as shall develop in them the largest capacity for performing the duties of American citizens.

3. To cherish, maintain and extend the institutions of American freedom, to foster true patriotism and love of country and to aid in securing for mankind all the blessings of liberty.

Membership

Section 1. Any woman, eighteen years of age or more, is eligible to membership provided she be descended from a man or a woman who, with unfailing loyalty, rendered material aid to the cause of American Independence; or from a recognized patriot, soldier or sailor or Civil officer, in one of the several Colonies or States, or of the United Colonies or States; and provided she be acceptable to the Society.

Section 2. An applicant for membership shall be endorsed by at least two members of the National Society.* The application shall be forwarded to the Registrar General and the initiation fee and annual dues (See Article IX) sent to the Treasurer General at the same time. The Registrar General shall report on the eligibility of the applicant to the National Board of Management and the application shall be voted on by ballot. If the majority of said Board approve such application, the applicant shall be declared a member of the National Society.

Section 3. If the applicant present a card of transfer from the National Society of the Children of the American Revolution, showing that she was in good standing with all dues paid to that Society to the age of eighteen, and the transfer be given within a year thereafter, she shall be admitted to the National Society and be exempt from payment of the initiation fee, if eligible to the National Society of the Daughters of the American Revolution.

Section 4. All persons whose applications were approved on or before October 11, 1891, are charter members of the National Society.

---

* It was voted at the Twenty-first Continental Congress, that the application papers of those wishing to become members-at-large must be endorsed by the Regent of the State in which the applicant resides.

THE NATIONAL SOCIETY OF THE SONS OF THE AMERICAN REVOLUTION

Objects

The purposes and objects of this Society are declared to be patriotic, historical and educational, and shall include those intended or designed to perpetuate the memory of the men who, by their services or sacrifices during the war of the American Revolution, achieved the independence of the American people; to unite and promote fellowship among their descendants; to inspire them and the community at large with a more profound reverence for the principles of the government founded by our forefathers; to encourage historical research in relation to the American Revolution; to acquire and preserve the records of the individual services of the patriots of the war, as well as documents, relics and landmarks; to mark the scenes of the Revolution by appropriate memorials; to celebrate the anniversaries of the prominent events of the war and of the Revolutionary period; to foster true patriotism; to maintain and extend the institutions of American freedom, and to carry out the purposes expressed in the preamble of the Constitution of our country and the injunctions of Washington in his farewell address to the American people.

Membership

Section 1. Any man shall be eligible to membership in the Society who, being of the age of twenty-one years or over, and a citizen of good repute in the community, is the lineal descendant of an ancestor who was at all times unfailing in his loyalty to, and rendered active service in, the cause of American Independence, either as an officer, soldier, seaman, marine, militiaman, or minute man, in the armed forces of the Continental Congress, or of any one of the several Colonies or States, or as a signer of the Declaration of Independence; or as a member of a Committee of Safety or Correspondence; or as a member of any Continental, Provincial, or Colonial Congress or Legislature; or as a recognized patriot who performed actual service by overt acts of resistance to the authority of Great Britain.

Section 2. No one shall be entitled to membership in any State Society who has previously been a member of any other State Society and dropped for the non-payment of dues, until

United Spanish War
Veterans

Army and Navy Union
of the United States
of America

The Welcome Society
of Pennsylvania

Regular and Volunteer
Army and Navy Union

Sons of Veterans
United States of America

PLATE XIII

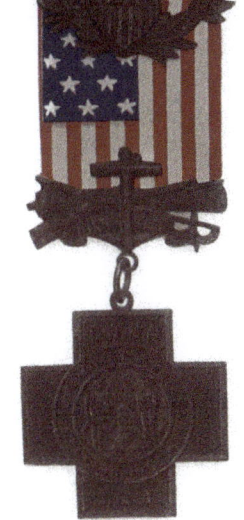

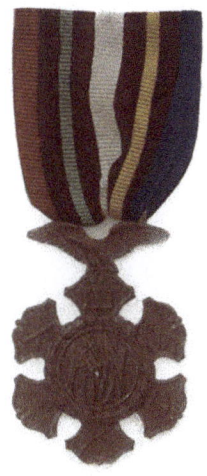

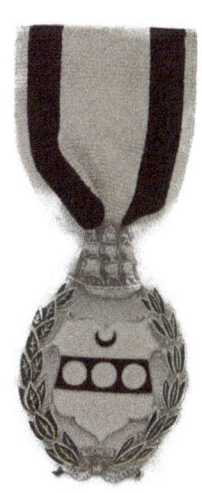

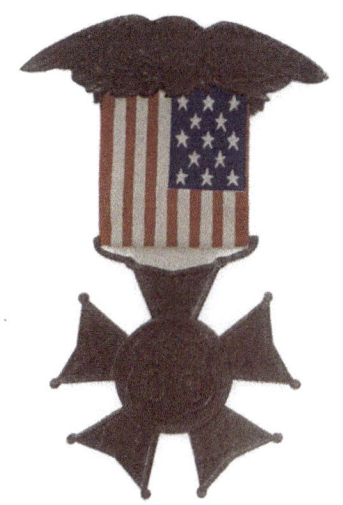

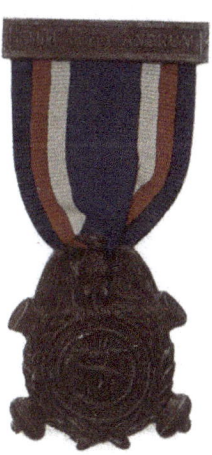

the indebtedness of such individual to the first Society shall have been adjusted.

Section 3. Applications for membership shall be made to any State Society, in duplicate, upon blank forms prescribed by the Board of Trustees, and shall in each case set forth the name, occupation and residence, of the applicant, line of descent, and the name, residence and services of his ancestor or ancestors in the Revolution, from whom he derives eligibility.

The applicant shall make oath that the statements of his application are true, to the best of his knowledge and belief.

Upon the approval of an application by the State Society to which it is made, one copy shall be transmitted to the Registrar General of the National Society, who shall examine further the eligibility of the applicant.   If satisfied that the member is not eligible, he shall return the application for correction.

Until the State Society shall satisfy the Registrar General of the eligibility of such applicant, his name shall not be placed on the roll of membership.

Section 4. The official designation of the members of The National Society of the Sons of the American Revolution shall be "Compatriots."

THE NAVAL AND MILITARY ORDER OF THE SPANISH-AMERICAN WAR

Objects

The objects of the Order are to cherish the memories and associations of the war with Spain; to promote ties of fellowship and sympathy among those who participated in the war, and to acquire and preserve the records of their individual services; to advance the best interests of the sailors and soldiers of the United States; to promote unqualified allegiance to the general government; to protect the rights and liberties of American citizenship; and to maintain the national honor.

Membership

Section 1. Any man of good repute shall be eligible to membership in the Order who was on the active list, or performed active duty (and who is still in the service, or has received an honorable discharge from the same) as a commissioned officer, regular or volunteer, in the United States Army, Navy or Marine Corps, or as a contract surgeon, during the war with Spain, or in the subsequent insurrection in the Philippines prior to April 1, 1901; or participated in the said war or insurrection, prior to said date, as a midshipman, naval or military cadet, or as an officer in the United States Revenue Cutter Service on any vessel assigned to duty under the control of the United States Navy Department, or as a warrant officer, non-commissioned officer, or enlisted man, and subsequently became a commissioned officer in the United States Army, Navy or Marine Corps.

Section 2. Upon the death of a Companion of the Order, or officer eligible to membership by right of personal service in the Spanish-American War, or in the insurrection in the Philippines prior to April 1, 1901, all his direct male lineal descendants reaching the age of twenty-one years shall be eligible for election as Companions of the Order, or by Inheritance.

Provided, First. That the inheritance shall in every case of succession be traced anew from the original founder of the membership in the Order, or deceased officer as aforesaid, and not otherwise, and shall be limited in cases of collateral succession to the brothers, and descendants of brothers and sisters, of such Original Companion or deceased officer; in cases of representation through females, the elder branches shall be preferred to the younger.

Second. That any person eligible to membership by inheritance, or by renunciation of another, may, in writing, waive and renounce his right to such eligibility in favor of the person next entitled at the time of such renunciation, excepting that no person who is a direct lineal descendant of an Original Companion or deceased officer as aforesaid shall be allowed to waive his right in favor of a collateral relative of such Original Companion or deceased officer.

Third. That in case a companion, or person already eligible to membership, is next in line of inheritance from an Original Companion or deceased officer as aforesaid, the eligibility to membership derived from such deceased Companion or officer shall devolve upon the person next entitled other than such living Companion or person already eligible, or the direct lineal descendant of either; but any Original Companion having no direct lineal descendant may, by writing filed with the Recorder of the Commandery in which he may be enrolled, or by his last will and testament or instrument in the nature thereof, nominate for life his successor from among his male heirs within the said limits in the collateral branches of his family.

Fourth.   That in cases of inheritance by persons under the age of twenty-one years the right of succession to eligibility to membership, or of renunciation thereof, shall remain in abeyance until they shall attain that age.

Fifth.   That the resignation, expulsion, or forfeiture of membership of a Companion who has obtained such membership by inheritance, or the rejection by the Commandery of an applicant for membership whose claim thereto is based on inheritance, shall only work as a waiver of his rights in favor of the next person in line of inheritance from the Original Companion or deceased officer as aforesaid.

Sixth.   That no right of inheritance shall be derived from any Original Companion whose membership in the Order was forfeited under Article XVII of the Constitution, and who was not reinstated.

Section 3.   The direct male lineal descendants, twenty-one years of age, of living Companions, whether original, by inheritance or in succession, shall be eligible to election as Junior Companions.   Upon the death of the Companion from whom he derives eligibility, a Junior Companion shall become a Companion in Succession.

Section 4.   A Companion having no direct lineal male descendants may nominate for election as Junior Companion a male member of his family descending only from his brother or sister. If the nominee shall be a minor, the nomination shall remain in abeyance until he reaches the age of twenty-one years. A Junior Companion so elected shall become a Companion in Succession upon the death of the Companion who made the nomination, provided, that if a Companion shall have descendants subsequent to his nomination of and the consequent election of a Junior Companion, the future representation of the family in the Order shall revert to the direct line and succession in the collateral line following the nomination and election shall terminate. In case a nomination be not made by a Companion having no direct lineal male descendants, the eligibility shall follow the rule laid down in Article III of the Constitution, in the collateral branches of his family in the order of genealogical succession.

THE ORDER OF COLONIAL LORDS OF MANORS IN AMERICA

Objects

The study of feudal institutions in the Colonial period of American History; to collect and publish all that can be gleaned in public and private archives, manuscript and otherwise, relating to Manor lands; to locate and secure photographic copies of portraits of Lords and Ladies of Manors; to bring to light the laws covering the rights and privileges and obligations of Lords of Manors in England in the 17th and 18th centuries, and thus contribute an unwritten page in the history of the American Colonies when feudal institutions were under English Rule and Custom.

Membership

Membership, which is limited, is by invitation in the name of "The Order of Colonial Lords of Manors in America," and is in right of descent from a man or woman who enjoyed feudal rights in any of the American Colonies prior to July 4th, 1776; as a Proprietary, a Lord of a Manor, a Patroon, a Landgrave, or by whatever designation known, enjoying equal rights and privileges.

THE ORDER OF THE CROWN OF AMERICA

This honorary organization, whose work dates from 1898, and whose Constitution was issued in 1902, was founded by Miss Henrietta Lynde de Neville Farnsworth, of Detroit, Michigan.

Its purpose is to perpetuate the memory, not only of illustrious Colonial ancestors, but of those belonging to earlier generations who descended lineally and legitimately from the royal houses of the old world; to keep in mind the efforts made by them towards the furtherance of human progress; to encourage the acquisition of knowledge relating to the periods in which they lived, and to inspire the loftiest conceptions of American citizenship.

Membership

Membership shall be by invitation only, such invitation to be extended by State Councilor through the State Secretary

Military Order of
Moro Campaigns

National Society of
Americans of Royal
Descent

National Society of
Daughters of Founders
and Patriots of America

Scions of
Colonial Cavaliers

The Holland Society
of New York

PLATE XIV

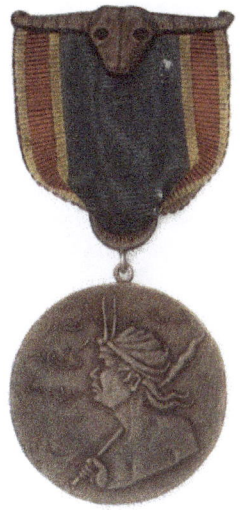

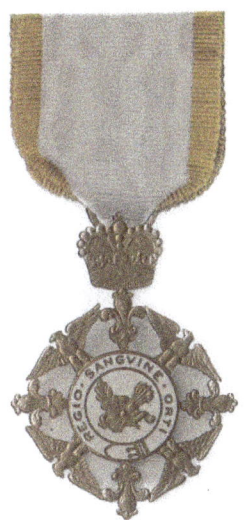

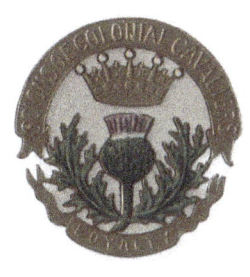

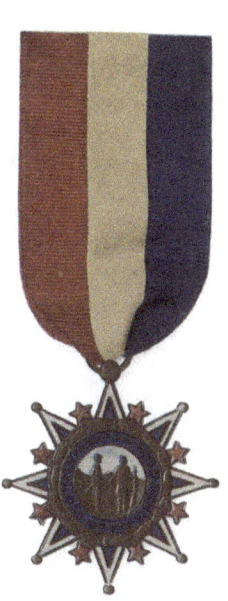

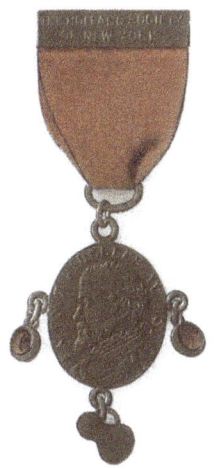

upon request of two members, one of whom is personally acquainted with the proposed Candidate. With the invitation, the State Secretary will enclose to the applicant Application and Lineage Blanks to be filled out by the Applicant and forwarded by her direct to the President General. She will file one set of these papers in the Temporary Case and send the other to the Registrar General, whose duty it shall be to carefully examine same, and if satisfied of the Applicant's eligibility and desirability, she will file papers and report to the President and Secretary General. The latter will in turn notify the Applicant.

The Applicant is allowed two months in which to accept, this acceptance to be sent to the Secretary General with Initiation Fee and Dues for first year. She, in turn, will forward Fees and Dues to the Treasurer General. The latter will send to the President General name and address of new member.

The lineage record must be made out and signed by a professional genealogist of recognized standing.

THE ORDER OF THE FOUNDERS AND PATRIOTS OF AMERICA

Objects

The Order of the Founders and Patriots of America, as its name indicates, lays emphasis upon two heroic classes—the Founders, the brave pioneers who in the Seventeenth Century came to and subdued the primeval wilderness of the American Continent, establishing here the civilization which has developed so gloriously; and the Patriots, those who in the years of the Revolution played an immortal part in the cause of liberty. No other hereditary society combines both these fields. The need for an Order whose insignia should be the badge of the double honor of a descent from both Founders and Patriots was recognized, and this Order was organized in 1896. Its remarkable growth and success have demonstrated the reality of this need. There are now six State Societies under the General Court, the New York, organized April 24th, 1896; the New Jersey, organized April 28th, 1896; the Connecticut, organized May 9th, 1896; the Pennsylvania, organized January 14th, 1897; Massachusetts, organized May 29th, 1914; the Illinois, organized October 8th, 1914. Although the conditions of eligibility are necessarily very strict, there are about seven hundred and seventy members of the Order; and the Pennsylvania Society has at present one hundred members.

Membership

Section 1. Any man of the age of twenty-one years, of good moral character and reputation, and a citizen of the United States, who is lineally descended, in the male line of either parent, from an ancestor who settled in any of the Colonies now included in the United States of America, prior to May 13, 1657, and one or all of whose intermediate ancestors, in the same line, who lived in the period of the Revolution, from 1775 to 1783, adhered as patriots to the cause of the Colonies, shall be eligible to membership in the Society, except as hereinafter provided. Provided always, That the Society reserves to itself the privilege of rejecting any nomination that may not be acceptable to it.

Section 3. The male descendants of any associate, being of good moral character and reputation, and citizens of the United States, shall also be eligible to membership, provided that the claims of each such descendant shall be traced anew from the qualifying ancestor from whom the first associate was eligible.

The clause in Section 1, "Adhered as patriots to the cause of the Colonies," means attachment to the cause of the Colonies shown by military or naval service against Great Britain or affirmative, public and consistent acts manifesting adherence, and loyalty to the American cause in the American Revolution. This must be satisfactorily proved by proper evidence.

THE ORDER OF THE GOLDEN HORSESHOE OF TRAMONTANE

This Order has a Charter from the College of Arms of Canada, with right of registry of those of its members for privileges of Noblesse under the Crown in Canada, etc., who conform to the requirement of such registry under the edict of 1760, which requires descent in the male line, family name from a Royal Officer, military or civil, of 1760, or before, of honorable European ancestry, or from an officer of the United Empire

Loyalist List of 1783, of limited European ancestry, by special provision of the Loyalist Act of Quebec, of King George III.

Membership

They must be descended from one of the 60 Knights of this Order, created in 1716 by the Royal Governor of Virginia, Sir Alexander Spottswood, for their achievement of opening and defending the territory of Tramontane for King George II, west of the Blue Ridge (now Kentucky, Southern Orio and Indiana).

THE ORDER OF THE WHITE CRANE

Object

To unite the family of mankind into one family, so far as regards brotherly love, justice and well-being, into a band of Christian Knights.

Membership

All those who descend from the native Chiefs of America, together with all those who descend from Colonial Ancestry, who have been domiciled in America from the earliest period to the year 1783, and are of the Aryan Race (except as above specified as to the Indian Chiefs) or natives of the Americas, of Indian, Aztec or Toltec origin.

THE ORDER OF WASHINGTON

Founded 1895

History

This Order was founded at Mobile, Ala., in 1895, and, as far as I am aware, is the only one named for the illustrious general and statesman, George Washington. Our members having become separated, the Order remained in abeyance when an attempt was made by Mr. John Eyerman, of Easton, Pa., and myself, to revive the Order. The former having a die cast for the beautiful insignia now adopted by us, and also some handsome invitations issued, containing upon their face the necessary qualifications of admittance to the Order. Nothing further was done until I became permanently settled in this city, when I determined to reorganize the Order, and with the assistance of certain gentlemen, we placed it upon a firm basis, and on May 13, 1908, formally instituted the Order and received a Charter for the same on June 11, 1908, so that we have the satisfaction of knowing that The Order of Washington is now firmly established, and as a qualification for membership requires that the ancestor must have arrived in America before 1750, have been a landowner or founder of a town, held some official, military or ministerial position in the Colonial service, and had a descendant who aided the Colonies in attaining their independence.

J. G. B. Bulloch, M.D.,
Chancellor-General.

Objects

"Whereas, It should be the duty of all those of illustrious lineage to preserve intact the history and traditions relating to the foundation of their country, and to endeavor to promote peace, happiness, and the general welfare of mankind, therefore, we, the founders of this Order, should use our influence to see that our institutions are kept intact and free from pernicious influences and that freedom and liberty be promoted: Therefore, we whose names are subjoined do now institute an order of patriotism and chivalry to be known as The Order of Washington."

Membership

In order to become a member of this Order the ancestor must have arrived in America prior to 1750, have been a landowner or a founder of a town, and have held some official, military (naval) or ministerial position in Colonial days, and also had a male descendant who assisted the Colonies in attaining their independence.

In order to explain the above the following clause is offered:

The candidate to become a Companion in this Order must have descended in the male or female line from a male ancestor who assisted the Colonies in attaining their independence, and the revolutionary ancestor must have descended in the direct male line from an ancestor who was in the Colonies prior to 1750 and who or whose son held at some time an official position during the Colonial period, or, was a founder of a town, or, was in the military or naval service, or was a minister of the Gospel.

Imperial Order of the
Yellow Rose

Imperial Order of the
Dragon

Military Order of the
French Alliance

The United Daughters
of the Confederacy

National Association of
Naval Veterans
U. S. of A., 1861-1865

PLATE XV

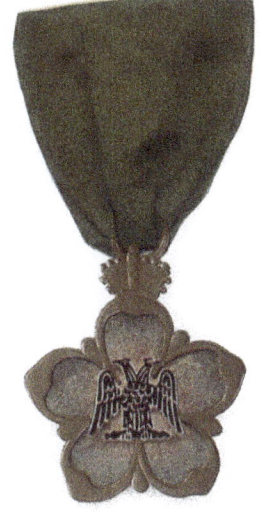

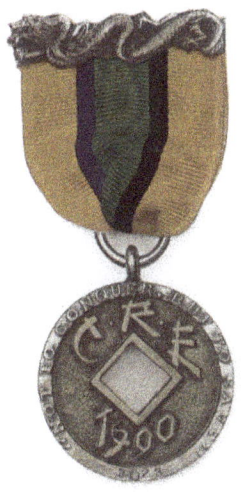

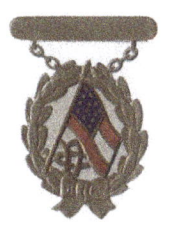

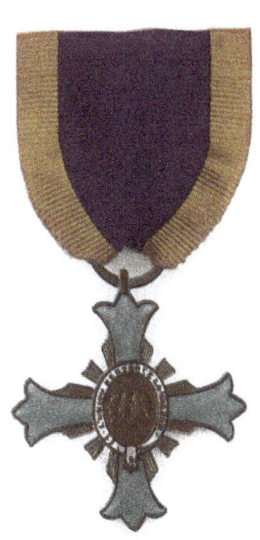

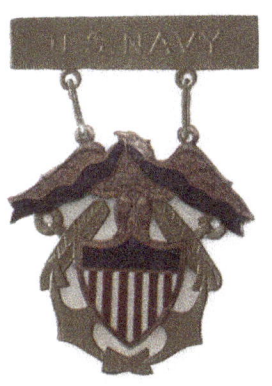

THE PENNSYLVANIA-GERMAN SOCIETY

Organized 1891

Objects

Section 1.   The objects of the Society shall be:

To perpetuate the memory and foster the principles and virtues of the early settlers in Pennsylvania of Germanic origin and of their descendants.

To bring to public notice and aid in the preservation of the landmarks and monuments of these early settlers and to collect and preserve the early printed records, books, papers, pamphlets, newspapers and in particular the documentary heritage, including manuscripts, letters, journals, church and church-yard records, and such other originals as relate to the history and genealogy of the Pennsylvania-Germans; and from time to time to publish them, especially such as will exhibit the part belonging to this people in the growth and development of American character, institutions and progress.

To set together the deeds of these early pioneers in the American wilderness in connected historical form, and give them a permanent place in American literature.

To cause statedly to be prepared and read before the Society papers on the history, biography, genealogy, customs, language, art and folklore of the Pennsylvania-Germans.

To promote social intercourse among its membership.

Membership

Section 1.   The membership of the Society shall consist of three classes, viz.: Regular, Associate and Honorary.

Section 2.   Regular members shall be direct descendants of early settlers in Pennsylvania of Germanic origin.

Section 3.   Associate members shall be any Americans of German descent, or any Germans who have become naturalized citizens of the United States, or, any persons who are in sympathy with the objects of this Society. They shall be entitled to all the rights and privileges of members, except that they shall have no vote and shall be ineligible to hold office.

Section 4.   Honorary membership may be conferred upon distinguished persons who are in sympathy with the objects of the Society and who have won eminence by their learning or achievements in matters pertaining to the objects of the Society.

Section 5. Applications for membership of all classes shall be made in writing on blank forms, to be supplied by the Secretary, which shall be signed by the applicant and by two members of the Society, and shall contain the date and the place of birth, the occupation of the applicant and the line of ancestry from which the applicant has descended, together with such other data as the blank form may indicate, or which the Executive Committee may from time to time require. All applications for membership that may be presented to the Executive Committee at any of its meetings shall lie over and be acted upon at its next meeting; and if the application be found in order and accompanied by the dues, as provided in Article IV, Section 1, hereof, the applicant shall be balloted for, and a two-thirds affirmative vote of the members present shall be necessary to elect.

Section 6. Life members shall consist of such Regular or Associate members as may be elected to this class by the Executive Committee and as have conformed to the requirements of Article IV, Section 2, hereof.

Section 7. Honorary members shall be nominated by the Executive Committee and elected by the Society.

Section 8. The nineteen gentlemen who attended the two preliminary meetings at Lancaster, Pennsylvania, February 14 and February 26, 1891, to organize the Society shall be known as "Founders."

THE PILGRIM SOCIETY

Incorporated 1820

Object

The landing of the Pilgrims at Plymouth in the month of December, in the year 1620, and the permanent foundations laid by them in Church and Commonwealth under peculiar circumstances of privations and toil, are among the first lines of the history of New England and of these United States. Their various emigrations from the north of England, the land of their nativity, to Amsterdam and to Leyden, in Holland, in 1607 and

1609, and their final removal to America, in 1620, as above stated, are remarkable eras in their pilgrimage, the commemoration of which has become an anniversary piously celebrated on the 22d day of December by their descendants.

That these historical events should be perpetuated by durable monuments, to be erected at Plymouth, is a desirable object in which public feeling very laudably concurs, and which has led to the institution and incorporation of the Pilgrim Society.

Membership

Any person of good moral character, who shall have paid into the treasury for the use of the Society, the sum of five dollars (or any person who shall have paid or shall pay the sum of five dollars in aid of the proposed monument to be erected in honor of the Pilgrims), and obtained a certificate or receipt from the Treasurer, or, in his absence, from the Recording Secretary, for the said sum, shall be entitled to membership, and the Secretary shall, on receipt of such document, deliver to every such person a diploma accordingly.

Any person of respectable character may be proposed as a candidate for honorary membership at any meeting of the Society, and if a majority of votes be given in his favor, he shall be admitted as an honorary member.

Any person who shall present to the Library or Cabinet any article or articles which the Trustees shall deem sufficiently valuable to entitle him to membership, may be then admitted as a member.

THE ST. NICHOLAS SOCIETY OF THE CITY OF NEW YORK

Organized February 28th, 1835. Incorporated April 17th, 1841

Objects

To collect and preserve information respecting the history of the City of New York and to promote social intercourse among its native citizens, as well as to engage in certain relief work.

Membership

Any person of full age in respectable standing in society, of good moral character, who was a native or resident of the city or State of New York prior to the year 1785, or who is the descendant of any such native or resident, or who is a descendant of a member of this Society, shall be eligible as a member. But whenever, and as long as there shall be six hundred and fifty members of the Society no one shall be elected to membership unless he be the descendant in the oldest male line of a member or former member, and in all elections to membership the ballot shall be first taken on the candidates who may be the descendants of members.

THE SOCIETY FOR THE RESTORATION OF THE DUCAL PROVINCE OF NORMANDY

Divided into Five Branches—One in England,
One in Scotland, One in Ireland, One in Canada,
One in America

This Society is under Charter of the College of Arms of Canada, holding special privilege as the only College representing the ancient Crown of France by edict of Louis XIV, of 1664, and by recognition of the Crown of Great Britain in the Treaties of the Cession of Canada of 1760 and 1763. Rights of registration conferring privileges of Noblesse to those qualifying under requirements of the edict of 1760, are reserved to members.

Insignia

A shield gules with three leopards or. The shield is ducally crowned and suspended from a bar, on which are the words: "Norman de la Normandie." A scroll at the base of the shield bears the old Norman legend, "Dieu et mon droit."

Objects

To collect the records and armorial descriptions of Norman families—especially those of members. To associate together in a membership to practise and perpetuate Norman chivalry and traditions, especially derived from the Norman Conquerors. To urge forward the suggestion already made that the French Republic, in consideration that Great Britain will cancel the war debt due Great Britain from France, will cede the territory once known as the Ducal Province of Normandy back to the Crown of Great Britain with all its sovereign provincial rights as established by the Crown of France under Louis XII, when he received the Province from England under Treaty with the Estates of Normandy (Noblesse, Clergy and Burgesses), and which Treaty of Tenure has been violated by the French Republic, the constitution and Les Coutumes abolished, and the province erased and dismembered, shall be restored under the Crown of Great Britain and the ducal government remain as formerly.

That all descendants of the Norman race, however far removed, resent the present degradation of the hearthstone of their race and pledge themselves to do their best to restore its treaty rights aforesaid under guardianship of the Crown of Great Britain, whose constitution is also a derivative of that of Normandy.

Membership

Requires descent from the Normans and a pledge to aid in restoring the ducal province.

THE SOCIETY OF THE ARK AND THE DOVE

Membership

Any person of legal age and of good, moral character and reputation is eligible for membership in The Society of The Ark and The Dove, who is lineally descended in the male or female line from Sir George Calvert, first Lord Baltimore, any of the gentlemen adventurers, or from any member of the company who came to Maryland in the ships "The Ark" and "The Dove" and assisted in the foundation of the Province of Maryland at St. Maries City, March 27, 1634.

THE SOCIETY OF THE ARMY AND NAVY OF THE GULF

Objects

To keep alive the many pleasant memories of the command, to foster among its members that kindly feeling and cordial companionship which characterized its officers in all their relations, to preserve the fair fame and glory of its fallen brave and to transmit to posterity the good name of the living while it faithfully cherishes the memory of its dead.

Membership

Officers of the Army and Navy who served in the Department of the Gulf, and have been honorably mustered out, or who still remain in the Army and Navy of the United States. Honorary members may be elected from time to time from officers who have served in the Armies and Navies of the United States.

THE SOCIETY OF THE ARMY OF GEORGIA

Instituted December 15th, 1868

Objects

The object of the Association shall be to preserve and perpetuate the history of the Army of Georgia; to preserve and unite those patriotic sentiments, and to maintain and strengthen that courteous and friendly intercourse for which the members of this army have always been distinguished; to preserve the name and fame of the members of this army, who have fallen in the field, or who have otherwise perished in the service of their country, shall be one of the sacred duties of this Association, and no efforts shall be spared to collect and preserve in the archives of the Society, the testimonials of their deeds and services.

This Society tenders to the widows and orphans of our fallen comrades its warmest sympathy, and readily pledges itself to provide for the wants and relieve the suffering of all such of them as are destitute, by the voluntary contribution of its members, or in such other way as from time to time may be determined.

It further pledges itself to use all proper effort to procure for all such disabled soldiers, and their families, as are entitled thereto, the pensions and bounties now provided by law.

The welfare of the soldier's widow; the good name and education of his children, shall always be regarded as a sacred privilege and trust of the Association.

Membership

All such officers and soldiers as have at any time served in this army, and who have been honorably discharged from such service; or who remain in service in the regular army, who shall have subscribed to the Constitution and By-Laws of the Society.

Honorary members may, from time to time, be elected from among the officers of other armies of the United States, who have served with distinction in their armies.

THE SOCIETY OF THE ARMY OF THE JAMES

Information as to Objects and Requirements for Membership not available at time of publication.

THE SOCIETY OF THE ARMY OF THE POTOMAC

Organized July 5th and 6th, 1869, and Subsequently Amended

Objects

The object of this Society shall be to cherish the memories and associations of the Army of the Potomac; to strengthen the ties of fraternal fellowship and sympathy formed from companionship in that Army; to perpetuate the name and fame of those who have fallen either on the field of battle or in the line of duty with the Army; to collect and preserve the record of its great achievements, its numerous and well-contested battles, its campaigns, marches, and skirmishes.

Membership

Section 1. This Association shall be known by the name and title of "The Society of the Army of the Potomac," and shall include every officer and enlisted man who has at any time served with honor in that Army, and been honorably discharged therefrom, or remains in service in the regular Army, who shall have given his assent to the Constitution and By-Laws of the Society, and paid his initiation fee. It shall also include all officers and men serving on vessels which, during the war, were in active and immediate co-operation with the Army of the Potomac and who were honorably discharged therefrom or remain in the regular service, and who shall have given their assent to the Constitution and By-Laws of the Society and paid their initiation fee.

Section 2. Honorary members may, from time to time, be elected from those who have served with distinction in any of the other Armies, or in the Navy of the United States, and also from those who have acted as Orators and Poets at the Annual Reunions.

Amendment to Article I

Lineal male and female descendants of members of the Society of the Army of the Potomac and of deceased honorably discharged soldiers of the Army of the Potomac, who shall be of full age, shall be eligible for membership in this Society as second-class members and collaterals, and shall be entitled to all the privileges of membership save that of voting. The Executive Committee shall provide a badge and ribbon for second-class members distinct from that worn by first-class members.

THE SOCIETY OF THE ARMY OF THE TENNESSEE

Objects

The object of the Society shall be to keep alive and preserve that kindly and cordial feeling which has been one of the characteristics of this Army during its career in the service, and which has given it such harmony of action, and contributed, in no small degree, to its glorious achievements in our country's cause.

The fame and glory of all the officers belonging to this Army, who have fallen either on the field of battle, or in their line of duty, shall be a sacred trust to this Society, which shall cause proper memorials of their services to be collected and preserved, and thus transmit their names with honor to posterity.

The families of all such officers who shall be in indigent circumstances will have a claim on the generosity of the Society, and will be relieved by the voluntary contributions of its members whenever brought to their attention. In like manner, the fame and suffering families of those officers who may hereafter be stricken down by death shall be a trust in the hands of their survivors.

Membership

Every officer who has served with honor in the Army of the Tennessee, their wives, lineal descendants and other relatives.

The Union Society
of the Civil War

Society of
Colonial Dames
of America

The National Society
of the Sons of the
American Revolution

National Society
United States Daughters
of 1812

Daughters of the
Revolution

PLATE XVI

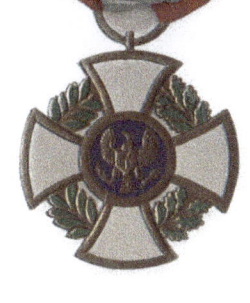

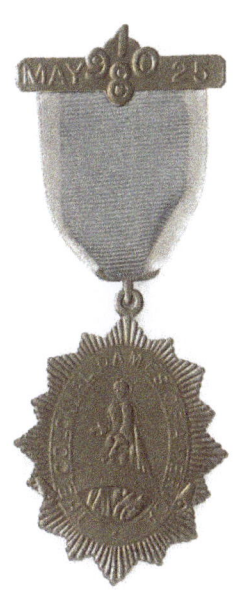

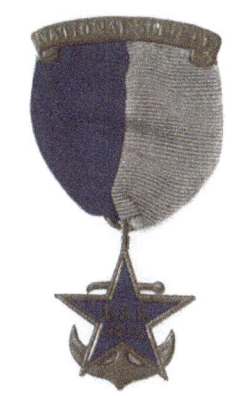

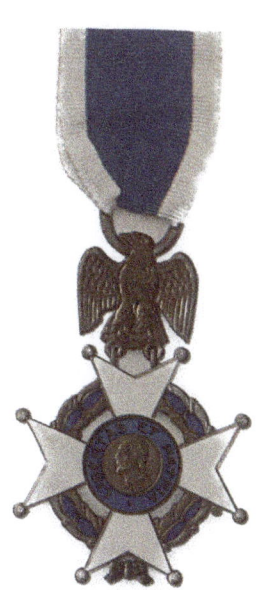

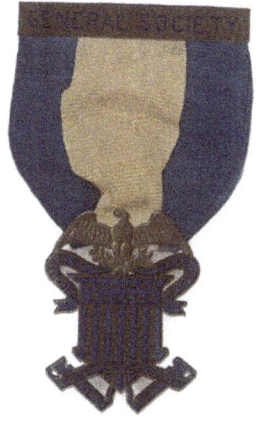

THE SOCIETY OF THE ARMY OF WEST VIRGINIA

Preliminary Organization, September 22d, 1870
Formally Organized, October 19th, 1871

Objects

To cherish the memories and associations of the Army of West Virginia; to strengthen the ties of fraternal fellowship and sympathy formed from companionship in the Army; to perpetuate the name and fame of those who have fallen either on the field of battle or in the line of duty with that Army; to collect and preserve the record of its great achievements, its numerous and well-contested battles, its campaigns, marches, and skirmishes.

Membership

The Association may include the Governors of the State of West Virginia previous to the close of the war; every officer and enlisted man who has at any time served with honor in that Army and been honorably discharged therefrom or remains in service in the Regular Army; also any officer and enlisted man living in what was the Department of West Virginia, but having served in other armies and having been honorably discharged therefrom. Honorary members may, from time to time, be elected from those who served with distinction in any of the other armies or in the Navy of the United States.

THE MILITARY SOCIETY OF THE WAR OF 1812

Organized January 8th, 1826

Consolidated with the Veteran Corps of Artillery of the
State of New York, January 8th, 1848

Objects

Whereas, The Congress of the United States, by Act approved June 18th, 1812, declared War to exist between the United Kingdom of Great Britain and Ireland and the dependencies thereof and the United States of America and their territories; and

Whereas, This appeal to arms by the American People, after unexampled forbearance, was made necessary by a continued series of hostile encroachments and aggressions on their rights, interests and territorial jurisdiction, and in defence of certain great principles of the Law of Nations which had been oppressively violated, for several years, to their great injury; principles which may be summarized as follows:

1.   That the Independence and territorial sovereignty of the nation is inviolable.

2.   That the National flag protects seamen on regularly documented American vessels against Foreign impressment.

3.   That the Neutral flag covers enemy's goods with the exception of contraband of war.

4.   That neutral goods, with the exception of contraband of war, are not liable to capture under an enemy's flag; and

5.   That blockades, in order to be binding, must be effective; that is to say, maintained by a force sufficient really to prevent access to the coast of the enemy and preclude a reasonable chance of entrance; and

Whereas, It is fitting that the principles for which "The War of Eighteen Hundred and Twelve" was waged by the United States should ever be borne in remembrance and upheld by the American People.

Therefore, This Military Society has been instituted by men who served in the Armies and Navies of the United States in the War of Eighteen Hundred and Twelve, to inspire among the members and among the American People the patriotic spirit of those who, in the military or naval service of the United States, or in service on private armed vessels of the United States, bearing commissions of letters of marque and reprisal from the United States, during the War, defended their Country against hostile encroachments on its rights and interests and caused its sovereignty and independence to be respected; to inculcate and maintain the great principles of the Law of Nations for which they contended, to collect and preserve the manuscript rolls, records and other documents relating to that War, and to commemorate the Land and Naval victories of the American arms in that War; to undertake and assist in the erection of proper memorials thereof; to perpetuate the mutual friendships formed in that War under the pressure of common danger, and to promote fellowship among the members of every degree; to participate in the celebration of other historic patriotic events of National importance, and generally to take such measures, patriotic, historical, literary, benevolent and social, as may conduce to the general intendment of this Institution, and better accomplish the objects thereof.

Membership

The members of this Institution shall be of two classes, namely:

Original or Hereditary, who shall be members in their own right, and

Honorary, who shall be members for their own lives without heritable succession.

Amendment to Article Governing Hereditary Membership, adopted October 18th, 1893:

On and after January 8th, 1894, eligibility to Hereditary Membership shall be restricted and limited to the proper descendants of Commissioned Officers, Aides-de-Camp and Commanding Officers of private armed vessels of the United States, comprehended and described in Section 1 of this article; and to the proper descendants of Original and Hereditary Members of this Institution heretofore duly admitted; and to the proper descendants of Original Members in military societies formed prior to January 8th, 1856, by men who served in the armies and navies of the United States in the War of 1812; and to Hereditary Members heretofore admitted in such military societies and their proper descendants; and to the proper descendants of the veteran delegates; and to the proper descendants of the veteran delegates to the national conventions of the soldiers of the War of 1812, held respectively in the city of Philadelphia on January 9th, 1854, and in the city of Washington on January 8th, 1855; provided, the actual military or sea service of the Original Member or propositus from whom descent is derived, were such as would have made him eligible to Original Membership in this Institution, and none other shall be eligible to Hereditary Membership.

Honorary Members

The President and Ex-Presidents of the United States, the Vice-President and ex-Vice-Presidents of the United States, the Judges of the Supreme and Circuit Courts of the United States, General Officers of the Army of the United States, not below the rank of Major-General, Flag Officers of the Navy of the United States, not below the rank of Rear Admiral, General Officers of the Society of the Cincinnati and Presidents of the State Societies of that Order, and Citizens who have received the formal approbation of the Congress of the United States for distinguished conduct or eminent services, shall alone be eligible to Honorary Membership.

THE UNION SOCIETY OF THE CIVIL WAR

Objects

The objects of this Society shall be to perpetuate the memory of those loyal officials who, outside the military or naval service of the United States, rendered invaluable aid and assistance to the National Government and Union Cause during the Civil War.

To unite and promote fellowship amongst them and their descendants; to encourage historical research in relation to the Civil War period; to acquire and preserve the records of the individual services of loyal Union officials of the War; as well as documents, relics and landmarks; to foster true patriotism and to maintain and extend the institutions of American freedom.

Membership

Section 1. Any loyal Union man who, between April 12th, 1861, and April 9th, 1865, served as President, Vice-President, Justice of the Supreme Court, Cabinet Officer, Minister Plenipotentiary abroad, Senator, Member of the House of Representatives, Special Commissioner, or Executive Secretary of the United States; Member, Associate Member or Chief Agent at the front of the United States Sanitary Commission; National Official of the United States Christian and Union Commissions or Chief Agent at the front; Loyal Governor of Loyal State; Lieutenant-Governor, State Secretary of State, State Attorney-General, State Treasurer, Commissioned Officer of Governor's Military Staff, President of State Senate, Speaker of State House of Representatives, Executive Secretary, State Executive Counsellor, Commissioned Officer of State Provost Marshal's Department on recruiting duty for United States Volunteer service; State Military Agent, Member of Commission, Board or Committee appointed by Governor to aid and assist in matters connected with national protection and defense; United States Military or Provisional Governor of Secession State.

Section 2. Also any male citizen is eligible for membership who received by name the "Thanks of Congress" for valuable services rendered to the National Government and Union Cause between April 12th, 1861, and April 9th, 1865.

Section 3. Any other Loyal Union man may also be elected to membership who, outside the Military or Naval service of the United States, between the aforesaid dates rendered services to the National Government and Union Cause which may be considered by the General Board of Managers to have been of sufficient value to warrant his election to membership in the Society.

Section 4. Any man twenty-one years of age is eligible for membership who is descended from any of the foregoing persons, provided he may be found worthy.

THE UNITED DAUGHTERS OF THE CONFEDERACY

Objects

The objects of this Association are memorial, historical, benevolent, educational and social; namely, to honor the memory of those who served and those who fell in the service of the Confederate States; to record the part taken by the Southern women in patient endurance of hardship and patriotic devotion during the struggle, as well as untiring effort after the war in the reconstruction of the South; to collect and preserve the material for a true history of the War between the States; to protect and preserve historical places of the Confederacy; to fulfill the sacred duty of charity to the survivors of that war and those dependent upon them; to help educate the needy descendants of worthy Confederates; and to cherish the ties of friendship among the members of the Society.

Membership

Section 1. Those women entitled to membership are the women who are the widows, wives, mothers, sisters, nieces, grandnieces and lineal descendants of such men as served honorably in the Confederate army, navy, or civil service; or of those men, unfit for active duty, who loyally gave aid to the Cause. Also Southern women who can give proof of personal service or loyal aid to the Southern Cause during the war; and the lineal descendants or nieces of such women, wherever living. Northern women having no male relative who served the Confederate States of America in the War Between the States, 1861-1865, and having themselves performed no special service to same, but having married a Confederate soldier since 1865, and through this means becoming a member of the United Daughters of the Confederacy, shall have the words "by adoption" placed upon their certificate of membership, and upon the Registrar's books, and in all rosters shall be designated as members "by adoption." Said member being entitled to all the honors and privileges of this Association except that of holding any office in the General Association, divisions or chapters; except that of transmitting this honor to members of her family, only her children of a Confederate father; the honor dies with her if she has no children.

THE VETERAN CORPS OF ARTILLERY OF THE STATE OF NEW YORK

THE MILITARY SOCIETY OF THE WAR OF 1812 (q. v.)

Veteran Corps of Artillery Instituted November 25, 1790. In Service of the United States in 1812 and 1814-1815.	Military Society War of 1812 Organized January 8, 1826. Consolidated with Veteran Corps January 8, 1848.

Instituted November 25th, 1790

The Veteran Corps of Artillery, S. N. Y., instituted at the city of New York, November 25, 1790, exclusively by officers and soldiers of the War of the Revolution.

Organized as a separate and distinct Corps in the Active Militia of the State of New York, duly confirmed by the Governor of the State, March 8, 1791.

In military service of the United States June 25 to July 2, 1812, and September 2, 1814, to March 2, 1815.

Recruited after 1814, under authority of the Governor of the State, exclusively from Veterans of the War of 1812.

Corps regulations amended September 10, 1890, to admit descendants of Revolutionary Members or 1812 Veterans. Such limitations fixed by law, March 9, 1895.

Military Society of the War of 1812, organized at the City of New York, January 8, 1826, exclusively by Commissioned Officers of that War, regular and volunteer,

United with the Veteran Corps of Artillery, S. N. Y., January 8, 1848, as its Military Society of that War and Civic Association for Patriotic and other laudable purposes,

The Corps confirmed in statutory and prescriptive rights and privileges as a separate Corps in active militia, by Acts of Congress of May 8, 1792 (Section 1641 U. S. Revised Statutes), January 21, 1903, and May 27, 1908, and Acts of New York State Legislature of April 17, 1854 (Chapter 398) April 14, 1855 (Chapter 536), and March 9, 1895 (Chapter 91), April 13, 1904 (Chapter 328), May 15, 1907 (Chapter 350), and May 24, 1913 (Chapter 513),

Exemption from all jury duty conferred by Special Act of New York State Legislature of April 6, 1795 (Chapter 50).

Membership

Membership restricted and limited by law to those persons qualified by regulations in form of Constitution and By-Laws.

Extract from Constitution and By-Laws

Original Members

"Any defender of the country in the War of 1812, who served honorably in the Armies or Navies of the United States in that War, and who shall by reason of service be entitled under the laws of the United States to have his name placed on the pension rolls of the United States, provided that he shall have maintained since said War an honorable character."

Hereditary Members

"Restricted and limited to the proper descendants of commissioned officers, aides-de-camp, and commanding officers of private armed vessels of the United States, during the War of 1812; to the proper descendants of Original and Hereditary Members heretofore duly admitted. Representatives of Veterans of the War of the Revolution, under certain regulations as made and provided by the Council of Administration, may be admitted to the Artillery Service Detachment of The Veteran Corps of Artillery. (Under these regulations, members in good standing of the Society of the Cincinnati and of the Sons of the Revolution in the State of New York are eligible for membership in the Uniformed body.)"

THE WELCOME SOCIETY OF PENNSYLVANIA
Incorporated October 3, 1906

Objects

The purposes for which this corporation is formed are to perpetuate the memory of those who came to America in the good ship "Welcome," in company with William Penn, the founder of Pennsylvania, who arrived in October, 1682; to collect and preserve historic data relative to the settlement of the State of Pennsylvania and the founding of the city of Philadelphia, and to bring together in social intercourse and friendly relations the descendants of the aforesaid persons who came to these shores in the ship "Welcome."

Membership

Any person of good moral character and reputation, lineally descended from a settler who came to America in the ship "Welcome" in October, 1682, is eligible for election to membership.

UNITED MILITARY ORDER OF AMERICA

Incorporated 1915

Objects

1. To unite in bonds of fraternity and friendship the descendants of men in the Army, Navy and Civilian service of the North and South during the war between the states, and to promote patriotism.

Membership

Section 1. Any acceptable man, twenty-one years of age, shall be eligible to membership in this Order, who is an hereditary member or eligible to hereditary membership in a recognized Northern or Southern patriotic organization of the United States of America, in existence at date of formation of this Order, in which qualification for membership is based on military, naval or civilian service, rendered between April 12, 1861, and April 9, 1865, provided he is a lineal descendant in the male or female line of the person who rendered such service.

The foregoing membership clause only applies to Sections 1 or 2 of Article III, in the constitution of the Union Society of The Civil War, in effect on September 6, 1915.

UNITED SONS OF CONFEDERATE VETERANS

Organized July 1st, 1896

Objects

Section 2. The objects and purposes of this organization shall be strictly "Historical and Benevolent." It will strive:

Section 3. To unite in one general Confederation all Associations of Sons of Confederate Veterans, Soldiers and Sailors, now in existence or hereafter to be formed, and to aid and assist the United Confederate Veterans and all Veteran Camps.

The Order of the
Crown of America

Society of the Cincinnati

The National Society
of the Colonial Dames
of America

Daughters of the
Cincinnati

PLATE XVII

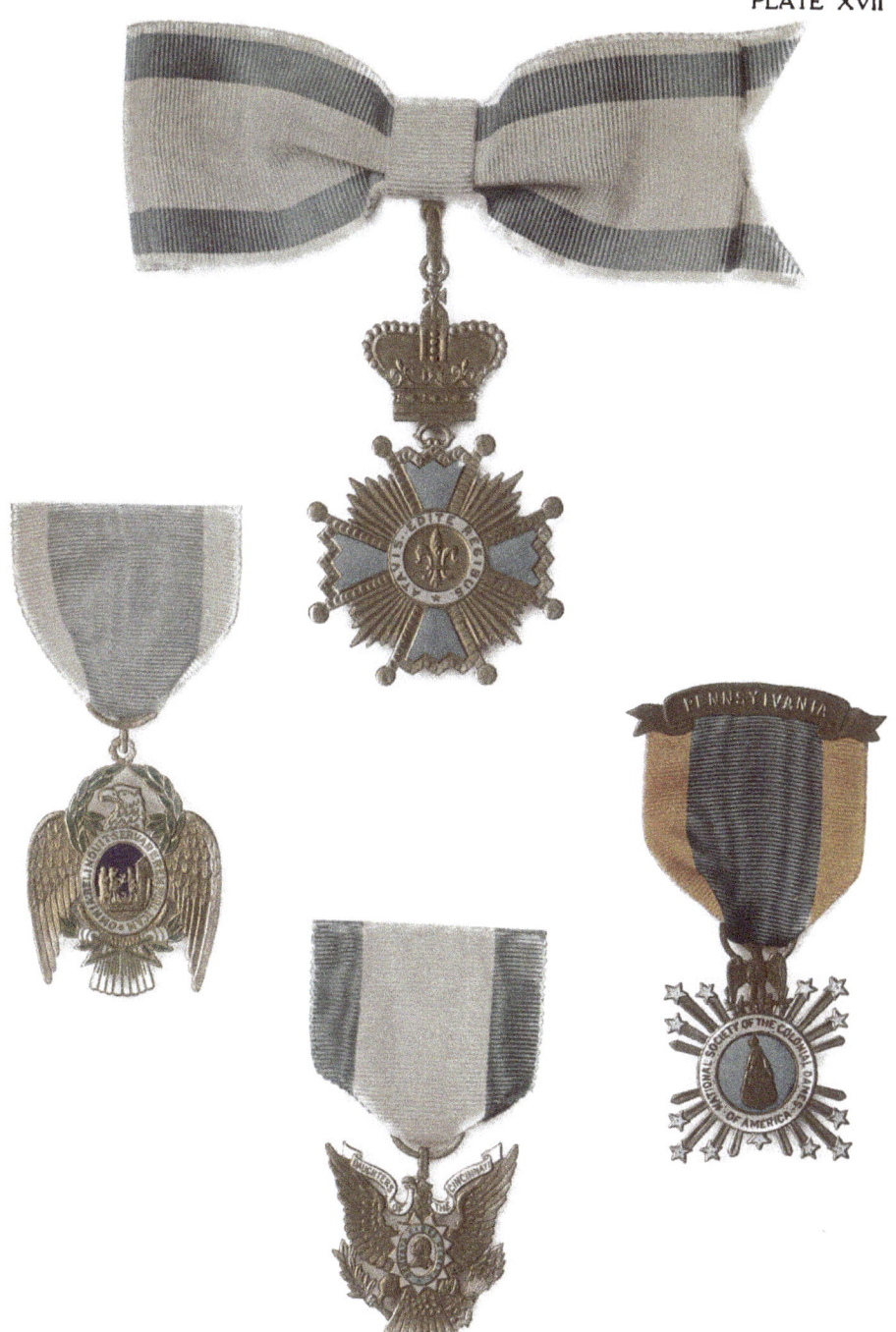

Section 4. To cultivate the ties of friendship that should exist among those whose ancestors have shared common dangers, sufferings and privations.

Section 5. To encourage the writing by participants therein of accounts, narratives, memoirs, histories of' battles, episodes and occurrences of the war between the States.

Section 6. To gather authentic data, statistics, documents, reports, plans, maps and other material for an impartial history of the Confederate side; to collect and preserve relics and mementos of the war; to make and perpetuate a record of the service of every member of the United Confederate Veterans, and all other living Confederate Veterans, and, as far as possible, of those of their comrades who have preceded them into eternity.

Section 7. To see that the disabled are cared for; that a helping hand is extended to the needy, and that needy Confederate Veterans' widows and orphans are protected and assisted.

Section 8. To urge and aid the erection of enduring monuments to our great leaders and heroic soldiers, sailors and people, and to mark with suitable headstones the graves of Confederate dead wherever found.

Section 9. To instill into our descendants a proper veneration for the spirit and the glory of our fathers, and to bring them into association with our Confederation, that they may aid us in accomplishing our objects and purposes, and finally succeed us and take up our work where we may leave it.

Membership

Section 11. All male descendants of those who served in the Confederate Army or Navy to the end of the war, or who died in prison or while in actual service, or who were killed in battle, or who were honorably retired or discharged, shall be eligible for membership in the camps of this Confederation, provided no member under sixteen years of age shall have the right to vote. Provided, no member shall be admitted under twelve years of age.

Section 12. No one shall be admitted to membership in any Camp until satisfactory proof of the foregoing qualifications be submitted in duplicate on official blank applications prepared for that purpose. The original shall be carefully preserved by the Camp, and the duplicate shall, within ten days, be forwarded to General Headquarters for record and permanent preservation. It is hereby expressly provided that all Camps shall, as far as practicable, bring together, on similar blanks, the records of all members, admitted prior to the adoption of this provision, one copy for the Camp and the other for General Headquarters.

UNITED SPANISH WAR VETERANS

Objects

The objects of the organization are to unite in fraternal bonds, through national, state and local organizations, those men who served in the military or naval establishments of the United States of America in the war with Spain, and in the campaigns incidental to and growing out of that war; to honor the memory, and preserve from neglect and oblivion, the graves of the dead; to assist former comrades and shipmates, their widows, orphans or dependent relatives, such as need help, encouragement and protection; to perpetuate the memories of the war with Spain and the campaign in the Philippine Islands and in China, and to collect and preserve the records of individual service of the members of this organization; to promote the best interests of those who took part in the war with Spain and the campaigns in the Philippine Islands and in China in the service of the United States; to inculcate the principles of universal liberty, equal rights and justice to all mankind, of loyalty to our country, reverence for its institutions, obedience to its laws and respect for its magistrates, and to discountenance whatever tends to weaken these sentiments among our people; to conserve national honor and union through unqualified allegiance to the National Government, and to protect the constitutional rights and liberties of American citizens. While requiring of every member of this organization that he shall perform his full duty as a citizen, agreeably to his conscience and to the best of his understanding, this organization is non-partisan, and must not be used for political purposes or the promotion of the candidacy of any person for political office, and no discussion of partisan questions is permitted at any of its conventions or meetings.

Membership

Officers, soldiers and sailors of the Army, Navy or Marine Corps of the United States of America, including acting assistant surgeons, contract doctors, dentists, and veterinary surgeons, all officers and enlisted men in the United States Revenue Cutter Service on vessels temporarily under the control of the War or Navy Departments, all officers and enlisted men in the Philippine Scouts and other organizations of native troops maintained by the War Department in the Philippine Islands, and Paymasters' clerks who were actually on duty in the field or aboard ship, who served at any time during the war between the United States of America and the Kingdom of Spain, or at any time during the war for the suppression of the insurrection in the Philippine Islands prior to July 4, 1902, and who either have been honorably discharged from the service or still continue in the same, shall be eligible to active membership in the United Spanish War Veterans; Provided, however, that no person shall be admitted to active membership who, upon investigation, is found to be of bad moral character or of low repute in the community in which he resides, or who having been honorably discharged from the service of the United States, has reentered the same and has subsequently received a discharge which is not honorable.

UNITED STATES VETERAN NAVY

Information as to Objects and Requirements for Membership not available at time of publication.

VETERANS OF FOREIGN WARS
OF THE UNITED STATES

Membership

Any officer, or any honorably discharged officer (including contract or acting assistant surgeon, dental surgeon or veterinary surgeon), or enlisted man who has served or may serve in the Army, Navy or Marine Corps of the United States of America, in any Foreign War (which definition shall be governed by the issuance of a campaign badge by the government of the United States of America) as the by-laws may provide, shall be eligible to active membership in the Veterans of Foreign Wars of the United States.

Under the by-laws the following are eligible:

1. Porto Rico. All who served in Porto Rico between April 21, 1898, and June 1, 1899.

2. War with Spain. All those entitled to Spanish Campaign badge for service in Cuba, Porto Rico, or the Philippines.

3. Naval Service. All those entitled to Philippine Campaign badge, China Campaign badge, Cuban Pacification badge, Nicaraguan Campaign badge issued by the Navy Department.

4. Philippine Service. All those entitled to Philippine Campaign badge issued by War Department for service ashore in Philippine Islands between February 4, 1899, and July 4, 1902; Department of Mindanao, Philippine Islands, between February 4, 1899, and December 31, 1904, and in the following Expeditions:

Against Pala and his Followers, Jolo, Philippine Islands, April and May, 1905.

Against Datu Ali and his Followers, Mindanao, Philippine Islands, October, 1905.

Against Hostile Moros on Bud-Dajo, Jolo, Philippine Islands, March, 1906.

In addition, several minor expeditions have been recognized as entitling participants therein to the Philippine badge. No compiled list showing all decisions under which these minor expeditions have been recognized is available, as each case presented is considered on its own merits. If any person believes himself entitled to a Philippine Campaign badge for service not indicated above, his application should be forwarded to the Adjutant General, War Department, Washington, D. C., when it will be considered in connection with such expeditions as are not listed above. If the applicant receives a campaign badge, he becomes eligible.

5. Boxer Rebellion. All those entitled to the China Campaign badge issued by the War Department for service ashore in China with the Peking Relief Expedition, between June 20, 1900, and May 27, 1901.

6. Cuban Occupation. All those entitled to Army of Cuban Occupation badge for service in Cuba with the Army of Cuban Occupation, between July 18, 1898, and May 20, 1902.

7. Cuban Pacification. All those entitled to Army of Cuban Pacification badge for service in Cuba with the Army of Cuban Pacification, between October 6, 1906, and April 1, 1909.

COLONIAL DAUGHTERS OF THE XVII CENTURY

Information as to Objects and Requirements for Membership not available at time of publication.

National Society Colonial
Dames, XVII Century

United Military Order
of America

Dames
of the Loyal Legion

National Society of
Colonial Daughters
of America

PLATE XVIII

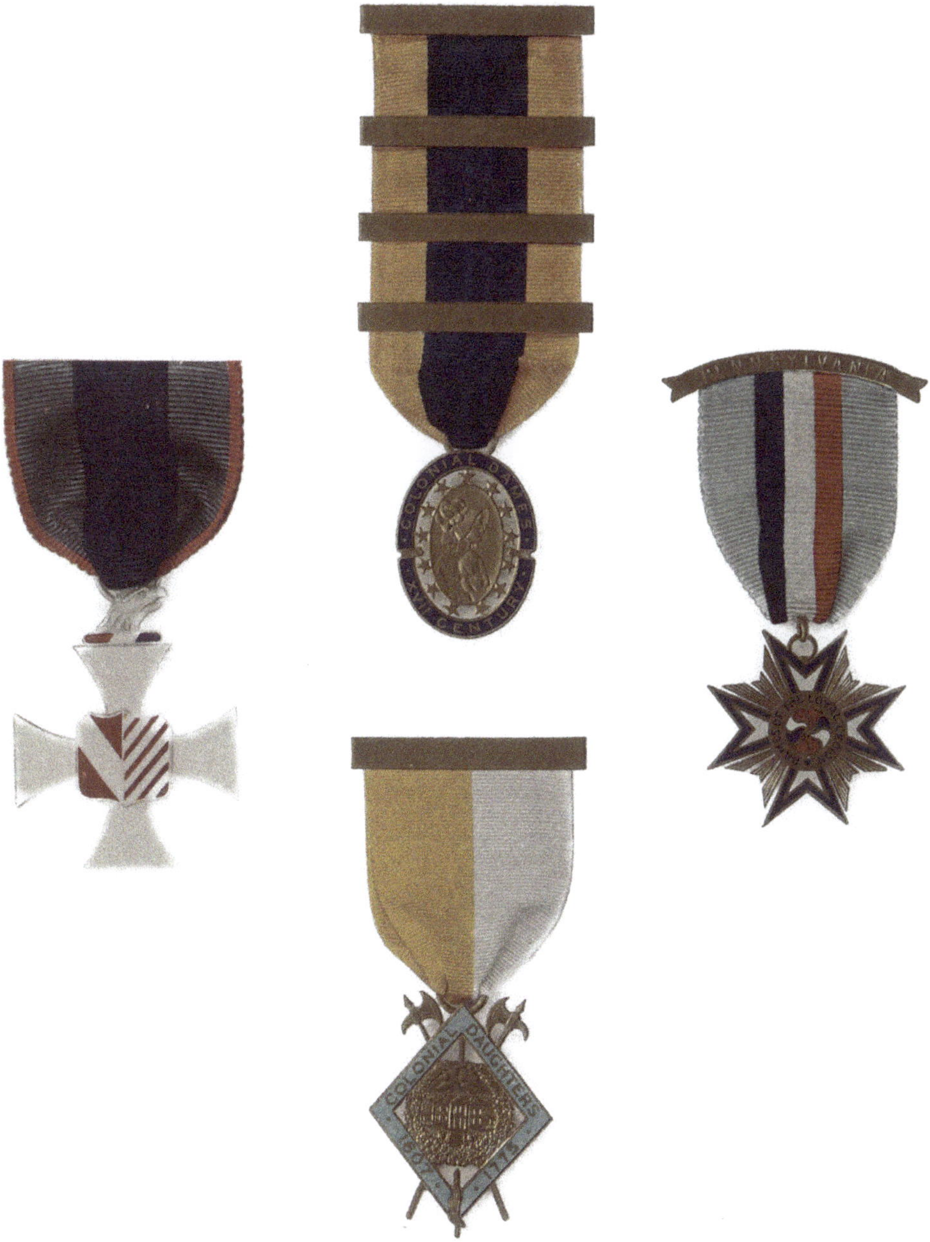

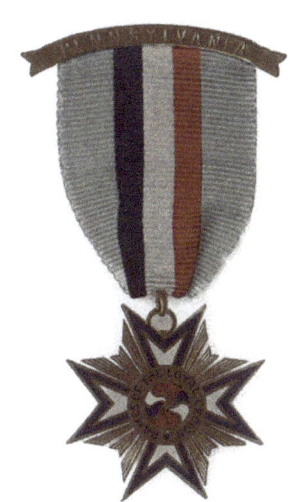

INDEX

The figures in the first column show the page giving the objects and membership requirements
The numerals in the second column give the plate number illustrating the insignia

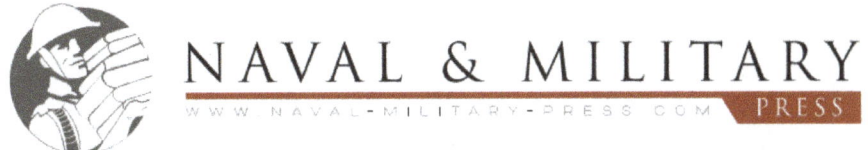

About The Naval & Military Press Ltd

Military book enthusiasts have a place on the internet dedicated to themselves. Our site is the most extensive devoted to military history on the web. You can browse and shop through our vast range of titles by time period or by theme, or use our advanced search facilities to find areas of specific interest.

The Naval & Military Press Ltd was founded in 1991 and quickly established itself as a mecca for the military enthusiast. Over 25,000 customers worldwide enjoy receiving our regular booklist which contains many hundreds of first-class books.

With the advances in modern technology we are now pleased to show all of you with access to the internet our full catalogue.

Our own publications feature strongly on both our list and our website. The innovative approach we have to military bookselling and our commitment to publishing have made us Britain's leading independent military bookseller

There is not another Military Book seller like
naval-military-press.com

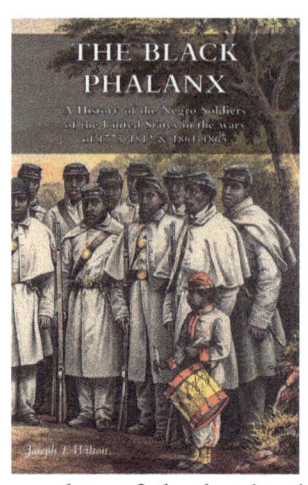

BLACK PHALANX
A History of the Negro Soldiers
of the United States in the wars
of 1775-1812 & 1861-1865
By Joseph T. Wilson
late Louisiana Native Guard Volunteers &
54th Massachusetts Regiment
The bulk of Wilson's compelling book concerns African Americans military service during the American Civil War, including the free Blacks who served in the Confederate army: "Descriptions of a number of the battles in which Negro troops took part in the late war of the Rebellion, are given to call attention to the unsurpassed carnage which occurred, and to give them proper place in the war's history rather than to present a critical account of the battles."

9781783315741

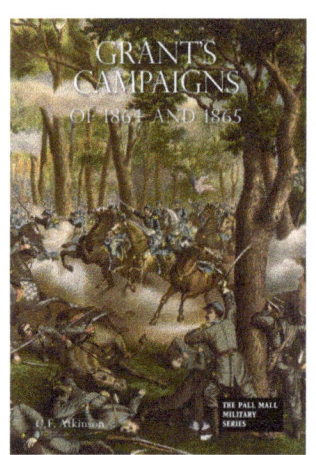

GRANT'S CAMPAIGNS
of 1864 and 1865 The Wilderness and
Cold Harbor (May 3 - June 3, 1864)
By Lieutenant C F Atkinson, 1st Batt. City of London (Royal Fusiliers)
This a detailed and scholarly account of Lee and Grant's first encounter. When the Grant's Overland Campaign ended, it left behind numbing losses: the dead, missing, and wounded totalled 55,000 for the Union and 33,000 for the Confederacy. Spotsylvania Court House (30,000 combined casualties) and the Wilderness (29,8000 combined casualties) were the third- and fourth-bloodiest battles of the American Civil War, trailing only Gettysburg and Chickamauga. The Confederate victory at the Battle of Cold Harbor would be one the war's most lopsided engagements.

9781783315635

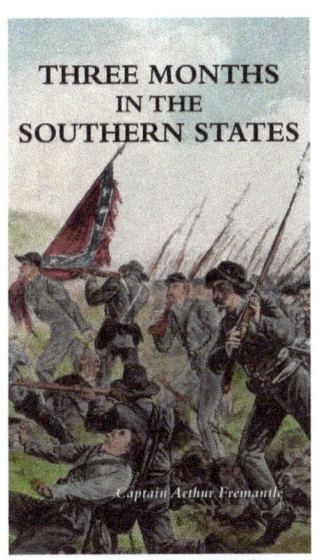

THREE MONTHS IN THE SOUTHERN STATES
April - June 1863
By Captain Arthur Fremantle, Coldstream Guards

A very interesting and detailed account of the officer's time with the Confederate forces of the South, Fremantle was a notable British witness to The Battle of Gettysburg, one of the bloodiest battles during the American Civil War. This is an important account that was a best seller when published in 1864, in both the North and South.

Most specifically mentioned in the book are Fremantle's travels through Texas, the deep south, and finally when he arrived in the company of the Army of Northern Virginia on June 27, and witnessed the Battle of Gettysburg firsthand, with of a cadre of foreign observers attached to the headquarters of Lt. Gen. James Longstreet. Contrary to popular belief, Fremantle was not an official representative of the United Kingdom; instead, he was something of a war tourist.

9781474539159

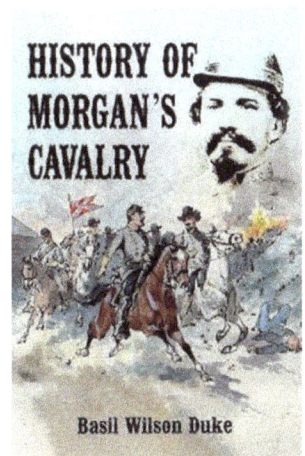

HISTORY OF MORGAN'S CAVALRY
by Basil Wilson Duke

Important account of General Morgan who served with the Confederate forces. This is a classic work about John Hunt Morgan's legendary exploits, written by Morgan's brother-in-law and a brigadier in his own right. The narrative describes many soldiers of Morgan's command in their adventures in Kentucky, Ohio, Tennessee and elsewhere. A focused military narrative of Morgan's operations, this work is valuable for Basil Duke's eyewitness recollections recorded so soon after the war.

9781474540797

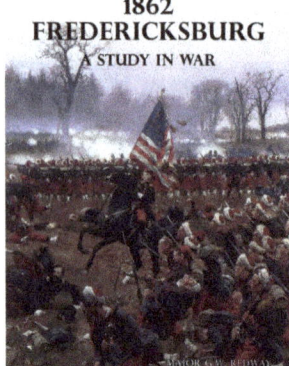

1862 FREDERICKSBURG
A Study In War
By Major G.W. Redway

Part of the acclaimed "Special Campaign" series of works intended for serious professional students of military history, each volume is interspersed with strategical and tactical comments and illustrated by numerous sketches.

Fredericksburg is remembered as one of the most one-sided battles of the American Civil War, with Union casualties more than twice as heavy as those suffered by the Confederates. A visitor to the battlefield described the battle to US President Abraham Lincoln as a "butchery".

9781783315444

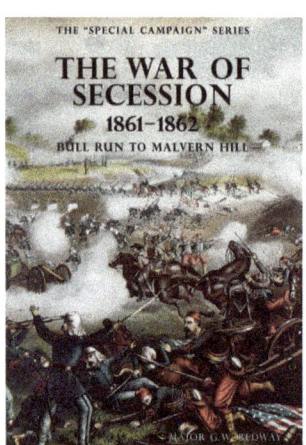

THE WAR OF SECESSION 1861-1862
Bull Run To Malvern Hill
By Major G.W. Redway

The American Civil War, known in Europe as the 'War of Secession', was marked by the ferocity and frequency of battles. Over four years, 237 named battles were fought, as were many more minor actions and skirmishes, which were often characterised by their bitter intensity and high casualties. As per the customs of the time, Prussian, French and British military observers were sent to the North American continent to observe the tactics of both armies, taking notes and reporting back to their homelands with observations and ideas about new tactics.

Covered in succinct chapters, Major Redway details subjects including: The Army System, The Command of the Seas, Organisation & Strategy, Tactics, Operations in 1866, Campaign in West Virginia, The Bull Run Campaign, Valley Campaign and Yorktown Peninsula.

9781783315482

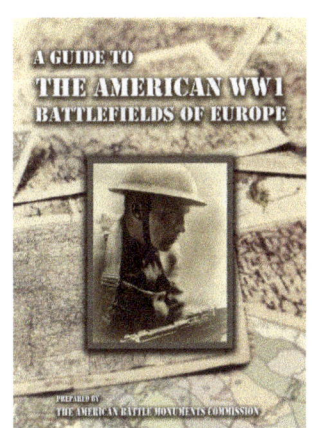

A GUIDE TO THE WW1 BATTLEFIELDS OF EUROPE

Prepared by the American Battle Monuments Commission

A solid reference for those who wish to know about the American evolvement in the Great War, and also good for family members discovering where a doughboy great-grandfather fought – this classic is a good place to start.

This 1927 guide is organised by region and campaign: Aisne-Marne, St. Mihel, Meuse-Argonne, Champagne, and the areas north of Paris including Flanders, Ypres, the St. Quentin Canal Tunnel and Cantigny. It includes narrative, photographs and maps.

9781474540483

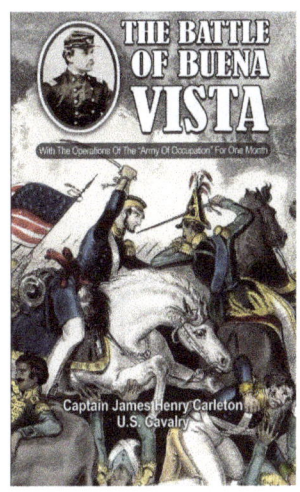

THE BATTLE OF BUENA VISTA
With the Operations of the
"Army of Occupation" for One Month
By Captain James Henry Carleton
U.S. Cavalry

This is the best account by a participant of the Battle of Buena Vista, the largest battle fought during the Mexican-American War of 1846-48, a war that was caused by the invasion of Mexico by the United States Army. It followed the 1845 American annexation of Texas, which Mexico still considered its territory. In the US this war was almost forgotten after the cataclysm of the American Civil War. The author Captain James Henry Carleton was an officer in the US Army and a Union general during the American Civil War. Carleton and is best known as an Indian fighter in the South-western United States.. Partly on the strength of 'The Battle of Buena Vista' he received an appointment from Secretary of War Jefferson Davis in 1856 to make a study of European cavalry tactics.

9781474540780

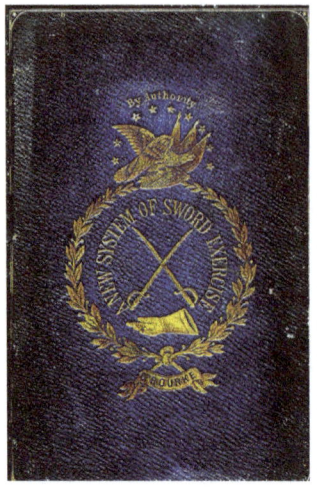

A NEW SYSTEM OF SWORD EXERCISE
With a Manual of the Sword for Officers,
Mounted and Dismounted
By Matthew O'Rourke Late
Captain US Volunteers

Illustrated with delicately clear line drawings, and first published on the eve of the American Civil War (this revised edition 1872) this Edged Weapon Manual tells the aspiring swordsman - mounted or fighting on foot - all he needs to know to defeat, wound and/or kill his opponent by the sword.

A must for the American Civil War, and Indian Wars Reenactor.
9781783312887

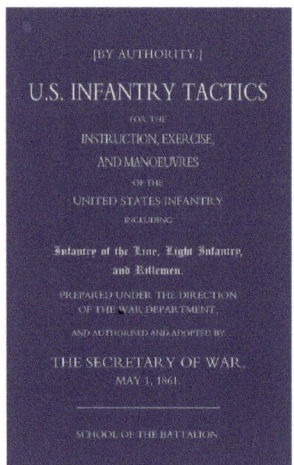

US INFANTRY TACTICS 1861
(SCHOOL OF THE BATTALION)
By Authority The Secretary of War
May 1, 1861.

On 20 April 1861 the Civil War in the United States opened with the capture of Norfolk Navy Yard by the Confederate forces from the South, and the war raged for four more years, with, as usual, the greater number of casualties being among the infantry. Infantry battle tactics were determined at the time by the firearms with which they were issued, and the main infantry weapon was the Springfield rifle musket. This muzzle loaded weapon was slow to fire, and marginally accurate, even with the new Minie ball: this meant that the tactics on the field of battle were almost unchanged from those of the Napoleonic wars, fought fifty years previously. This book shows how such evolutions (they were little more than drills) at battalion level were adapted and used to enable commanders to deliver the weight of their firepower on to the enemy.

All the prescribed manoeuvres could be practised on the drill square, so that once the men were in battle, all they had to do was obey orders, present their weapons and fire. Of course, all the drills in the world do not prevent panic, and records show that despite all the training, some men reloaded their weapons so many times without firing that the weapons were rendered useless. The book is extremely well illustrated with 67 plates of all the movements in plan form.

9781843426202

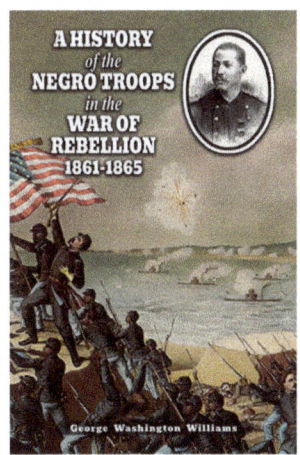

A HISTORY OF THE NEGRO TROOPS IN THE WAR OF REBELLION 1861-1865
By George Washington Williams

First published in 1888 this work is a major book-length academic history of the military history of African Americans in the American Civil War. Williams has been described as "the finest black prose stylist of his day" and this History showcases this skill.

This book has been called the most important of a trio of histories of 19th-century African-American military histories written by black authors, alongside William's Wells Brown's The Negro in the American Rebellion and Joseph T. Wilson's The Black Phalanx (This also republished by N&MP)

The author himself served enlisting at the age of 14, and fought during the final battles of the Civil War.

After the war, William's went to Mexico, where he was among Americans who joined the Republican Army under the command of General Espinosa, fighting to overthrow Emperor Maximilian. He was commissioned as a lieutenant, learned some Spanish, and earned a reputation as a good gunner. He returned to the U.S. in the spring of 1867,and reenlisted for a five-year stint in the Army. William's was assigned to the 10th Cavalry "Buffalo Soldiers" in the Indian Territory, but was wounded in a lung in 1868 and was hospitalised until his discharge that year.

9781474541312

www.ingramcontent.com/pod-product-compliance
Lightning Source LLC
Chambersburg PA
CBHW040107180526
45172CB00009B/1262